# French Letters and the English Canon

First published in the UK in 2007 by Timewell Press


A catalogue record for this title is available from the British Library.

ISBN-13: 978-1-85725-207-1

Typeset by e-Digital Design

Printed and bound in Great Britain by
William Clowes Ltd, Beccles, Suffolk

Timewell Press Limited
10 Porchester Terrace
London W2 3TL
United Kingdom

# French Letters and the English Canon

by Mark Daniel

(with contributions from Major Gilbert James George Larrison Moray Kilbride Constance Pumphrey, MC)

***Actualité*** – supposedly 'truth'. This gives us the opportunity to investigate at the outset a paradox about French words adopted into English. Everything French has always been regarded by the British as racy, naughty and even dirty, so, for example, condoms are 'French letters' and clap is 'French pox' (a sufferer is said to be 'Frenchified').

At the same time, French is widely thought of as 'refined' or even, in relation to brutish Saxonic English, euphemistic. So the huge majority of words branded 'non-U' by Sir John Betjeman and Nancy Mitford, and still indicative of ignorant aspiration, are of French origin where an English equivalent would have served – 'toilet', 'serviette' and the like. Characteristically, Hyacinth Bucket, the heroine of a sitcom about such aspiration, prefers to pronounce her surname 'Bouquet', while mutual oral sex is considered sanitised by the French *soixante-neuf*, although the number sixty-nine actually exists in English too.

*Actualité*, like its precise English equivalent, is not in fact widely used in French for 'truth' (*vérité*). It means rather something of current and immediate interest – the hot topic of the hour – or, in its commonest manifestation, 'news'. It entered the language at the whim of the late Alan Clark who, as a former Defence Minister in the witness box during the Matrix Churchill 'arms to Iraq' trial, admitted to being 'economical with the *actualité*', by which he meant, forked tongue firmly in cheek, that he had lied. Here he was adapting with spurious elegance a phrase – 'economical with the truth' – frequently used in the British House of Commons, where accusations of lying are wisely, if amusingly, forbidden. Recorded from the eighteenth century, this phrase was notably brought into contemporary usage by the UK Cabinet Secretary, Sir Robert Armstrong, who used the phrase during the Australian *Spycatcher* trial in 1986.

**Adieu** – a last 'goodbye' – has been part of the English language since the fourteenth century when it was correctly spelled 'adew'. The reversion to the original French spelling is needless and pretentious, but not so offensive as the resultant adoption of the French pronunciation (sort of), which resulted in that memorably ghastly rhyme in *The Sound of Music,* '*Adieu, adieu,* to yeu and yeu and yeu.' How Richard Rodgers must have mourned Lorenz Hart at that moment. *Adieu* is usually translated 'farewell' and the distinction is invariably made between *adieu* and *au revoir* or 'goodbye'. The distinction is etymologically false. *Adieu* does not mean, as I have seen it rendered, 'until God' (or 'see you at the Last Judgment'), but is derived from *A Dieu vous commant* or 'I commend you to God' (just as *adios* comes from *a dios vos acomiendo*), which, in essence, means nothing more or less than our 'God speed', 'Go with God' or 'Goodbye' (originally *godbwye* or 'God be with ye'). Nothing here, then, to indicate a terminal farewell. Of course, *au revoir, arrividerci* etc. stress the prospect of a reunion, but there is no parallel in common English usage aside from the irredeemably vulgar 'See ya' or 'TTFN' (ta-ta for now).

**Affaire** – surely by now an obsolete affectation, this form, though pronounced precisely the same as the English word, used to be used of love or, more precisely, sex affairs, whether brief squelching encounters between prostitutes and clients or enduring passions to shame Verona whippersnappers. The term, with inversion to ensure that we know the word to be French, persists to describe scandals of any sensational variety when journalists are bored with the meaningless suffix '-gate', so '*L'affaire* OJ Simpson' is used as a substitute for the even sillier 'Simpsongate' or the disgracefully straightforward, 'the OJ Simpson affair'.

The word 'afer' (plural: 'aferes'), meaning 'dealings or doings with' has been part of the English language since the thirteenth century, though heaven knows why. The divine Thomas Malory used the far more charming and identical 'ado'. His knights were always telling others, 'Hold, for I would have ado with thee', by which they meant neither, 'I wish to hold a party with you,' nor 'let us adjourn to that broom cupboard and there exchange bodily fluids', but, 'I would like to compete with you on the field of chivalry'.

**Agent provocateur** – a repugnant person who provokes, challenges or coerces suspected criminals or traitors into performance of illegal acts in order to secure a conviction or *casus belli*. Although Titus Oates of the Popish Plots of 1676 – 81 is perhaps the most notable and infamous British exemplar, having sent many innocent men to the gallows by reason of an intrigue concocted and encouraged by him, the phrase is thought to have entered the English language only in 1877. In a letter by W. de Horsey on 8 January of that year, we read, 'You may think that I am looking through very coloured spectacles when I attribute the Bulgarian atrocities to Russian intrigue ... that Russian *agents provocateurs* prepared the Servian rebellion ...' Although widely used of strike-breakers in the early twentieth century, the phrase is now principally known as the clever name of a notable maker of ladies' underwear.

**Aide de camp (usually ADC)** – lit. 'camp assistant' – no doubt very apt in certain regiments of the Guards and all-male magic acts. An *aide de camp* is a military officer appointed to work as a personal assistant to another of higher rank. The English must have adopted this phrase from the French in 1670 because of the close alliance between the two nations and their kings, Charles II and Louis XIV. Otherwise, it is unclear as to just why we could not have thought of one of our own.

**Aide mémoire** – lit. 'help memory'. Just what it says: a mnemonic, prompt, crib or other aid to memory.

**À la carte** – not, as might be supposed, 'from the trolley', but 'from' or 'on' the paper or menu. This dates from happier days when, on walking into an inn or *auberge*, the traveller asked what was for dinner, was told 'hotpot' or, as it might be, *pot au feu*, and sat down to enjoy the same fare as the proprietor's family and any other itinerant customer. Should our traveller have come from the twenty-first century, of course, he might object that he was allergic to mutton or had ethical objections to the consumption of potatoes, and would then be referred to a sheet of paper, whereon he would find alternative fare – no doubt terrines, soups and the like – listed, each dish, of course, with its own price. In due course, hoteliers and restaurateurs adopted this system, offering a *prix* *fixe* menu and a selection of other dishes on the *carte*. The great merit of this system was, of course, that the innkeeper was likely to be serving fresh, local, seasonal produce rather than esperanto garbage of dubious provenance. Since the Second World War, what with the growth of cheap democratic foreign travel and massively pollutant, pointless but profitable transportation of food, menus have extended to comprise not merely Shergarburgers, long-time-no-sea insulating fabric in batter and pies of Gobbets in Stuff in puffy bonnets, but a plethora of badly cooked dishes purporting to be Italian, Indian and so on. The *prix fixe* menu has all but disappeared, except, curiously, in the very best urban restaurants.

**Ambiance/ambience** – environment, the props and setting of a painting. From present participle *ambiens* of Latin *ambire*, to go round, so 'surrounding(s)'.

**Américaine, à l'** – a term with countless meanings, depending on the principal ingredient. Most commonly used, however, of lobster, first fried, then braised with tomatoes, shallots and brandy. If you think that this sounds so un-American as to require a visit from a SWAT squad and internment (or even interment) without trial, you are right. This is almost certainly a corruption of *à l'Armoricaine* – from Brittany.

**Amour propre** – self-esteem, a proper regard for oneself. The English, like all prudes, have filthy minds, and this is perhaps why the obvious 'self-love' was not adopted, though we must surely shudder when we consider just what people who thought thus made of the commandment that we should 'love our neighbours as ourselves'. Today, *amour propre* or self-esteem is a trendy virtue, much practised, and bragged of, and certainly more highly regarded than love of one's neighbour.

**Amuse-gueule** – literally 'amuse gullet' or 'mouth-tickler'. Generally, kickshaws or *canapés* served unsolicited and with no coherent relevance to the meal to follow because made with yesterday's leftovers, piled on croûtons and garnished or whisked up into frothy soups, dispensed, like medicinal syrups in hospitals, in precisely measured, minuscule doses.

**Ancien Régime** – the days before the French Revolution or the good old days, unless you are a bureaucrat or a ferocious knitter in need of diversion. Or, possibly, a horny-handed son of toil. Pumphrey, who arrived back here last night from Ibiza to assist in this work, says that French sons of toil do not have horny hands any more, but rely on bureaucrats to give them other people's money for doing nothing, but I would not even have mentioned this ridiculous assertion had he not been related to the publisher. Besides which, he has already hidden my nice pills.

**Angoisse** – our 'anguish' but, for once, describing an altogether less dramatic emotional or physical state than our version. 'Anguish', of course, is extreme pain, but *angoisse*, by association, perhaps, with the Dutch *angst*, dread, means a state of anxiety or fear occasioned by a stimulus unrecognised by the sufferer. Cyril Connolly, for example, complained of a persistent *angoisse des gares*, a niggling worry which afflicted him at railway stations. Now, the French do not do philosophy. They do a lot of talking and occasionally fighting about riddles which everyone else has long since resolved. So one day, arguing about whether existence preceded essence (as if anyone cared: Kant had sorted that one centuries earlier), one J.P. Sartre came up with a nonsensical thing called 'existentialism', in which *angoisse* figured largely, but there it meant the condition of a free being in a universe without absolutes. Christians had ceaseless *angst* or *angoisse* too. In Kierkegaard, it denotes the condition of a man or woman constantly concerned that his or her free will is causing him or her to disappoint God. All in all, *angoisse* is a fruitless state which can best be resolved by regular bowel movements, fresh air and sex.

**Apéritif** – not, as in the famous bad pun, a set of dentures, nor, as suggested by my foolish colleague, Pumphrey, who has simply refused to give me my medicine unless I include his views, 'a row with dad' (but then, the same unfortunate Pumphrey has also opined that *au bord de la mer* means 'fed up with mum' or 'on the town council' and *au bord de l'eau*, 'at the knocking-shop', which should make it plain that he is not a person of fitting seriousness for our purposes), but a drink to whet the appetite before eating. Another curious borrowing, because the English, like the French, had already taken on the word from the Latin. Our 'aperitive' meant 'a substance to open (*aperire*) the bowels' and dates from the sixteenth century at the latest. Perhaps it was these intestinal connotations, perhaps merely the medicinal sound and look of the word (as in 'carminative', say), perhaps the association of fine food and drink with France and the French language which caused the English to return to the French word in or around 1890, though we seem able to cope with 'Digestive' in biscuits.

**À point** – 'at the point'. Just enough. At the point of ripeness or fitness. In culinary terms, cooked to perfection.

**Après-ski** – 'after ski'. The time (and so the fashions and any activity pertaining to that time) at which skiers, having left the *piste*, go on it instead. Shaggy boots come into this quite a lot.

**À-propos, apropos** – literally, *à-propos* (the word exists in English as just one word) means 'to the purpose' or 'appropriate', and, when used without an indirect object, retains these meanings in English. 'I do not consider that remark to be apropos' is sufficient in itself, and it was in this form that the expression was first used, by the great John Dryden, in his *Essay on Dramatic Poesy* of 1668. As 'a propos of …' (*à-propos de …*), the phrase means 'with reference to …' or 'in respect of …'. Curiously, in its language of origin, the phrase principally means 'in good time' (we retain this sense in 'they arrived apropos'), or, as a noun, 'the timely, appropriate or "done" thing': 'L'à-propos est …'.

**Arabesque** – a swirling or curly line characteristic of Arabic decorative work, or a position in dance in which the dancer stands on one leg with the other extended backward and one arm forward and the other backward, like a pool player who has been goosed, mid-shot, and quite likes it. Also a richly ornamented, sometimes convoluted work of music.

**Argot** – slang of a peculiar class, social grouping or *métier*. Origin unknown. Originally underworld or street slang or 'cant', as it is properly known. Surely '*argot*' ultimately has the same origin as our own 'jargon', which comes from the same source as the French *gargoter*, to make a guttural noise.

**Arrière pensée** – 'behind thought'. An ulterior motive or 'hidden agenda'.

**Arriviste** – a noisome, ambitious, pushy, aspirant person.

**Attaché** – past participle of *attacher* so 'one attached'

– essentially an underling (often a spy) attached to the staff of an embassy or consulate rather than a functional member of the full-time staff, whence 'attaché case', a rectangular document case, once thought more secure than the standard briefcase, in which such a one might carry state secrets or sandwiches.

**Au courant** – 'Well, I know he's spent some time in France, so I'm sure he can be of some help,' the publisher said to me as he foisted his uncle Gilbert James George Larrison Moray Kilbride Constance Pumphrey, MC, late of the Royal Scots Greys, on me. Exactly how Pumphrey passed his time in France can be judged by his note here.

> *'Au courant: Well, of course, every French B&B claims to have this, but they wash so seldom over there that, when you turn on the taps, there's usually a bit of a splutter and a gasp which sounds like a dying astronaut and you're lucky if you get a Bishop's dribble of rusty water. Oh, and when it does work, their plumbers think it's funny to have hot water coming out of the tap marked "C". Just to get their own back for Waterloo, I suppose.'*

In fact, *au courant* means 'abreast of the latest developments', 'up to speed', and can, like this latter, be used suffixed with 'with' or on its own.

**Au fait** – Pumphrey (and we have already decided to ignore him) declares that this expression means, 'I have urinated'. Looking further down my list, however, he also maintains that *avoirdupois* is the infinitive denoting the same activity, and swears that French persons in bars have left his table, scowling and stating, '*Ooh, je dois avoirdupois*' and returned smiling broadly, announcing, '*Au fait.* Let's have another drink.' Pumphrey is actually a negligible person. In fact, *au fait* is used in English to mean 'familiar' or 'conversant', as in 'Pumphrey is not really *au fait* with French usage', or, on its own, 'expert' or 'in touch'. Although the first meaning – *au fait de* – exists in French, the expression is more usually used to denote 'to the point' or 'in fact'. This expression has been borrowed since the late eighteenth century by reason of its economy and brevity.

**Au naturel** – in French, *au naturel* can mean either 'in reality' or 'unseasoned' (in cooking). In English, we picked up the latter, less common usage and use it figuratively, to mean natural, untouched, pure, real or, of course, 'undressed' in a more literal sense than the culinary.

**Au pair** – does not mean, generally, or, at least, necessarily, 'at the or on the father' as Pumphrey suggests. Its literal meaning is 'at par', or 'on equal terms' – with the rest of the family, that is. Originally (1890s) an adverb describing such an arrangement, whereby a person lived not as a member of the domestic staff but as a member of the family in exchange for tutoring in a foreign language, it became a noun only in the 1960s.

**Auteur** – an author, but, today in English, a director who so stamps a film with his personality, style and conceits that he constitutes its *auteur* afresh. This barely ever applies in the era of films made by ignorant committees, but the likes of Hitchcock, Wilder *et al* so dominated their films, which were the better for it.

**Avant garde** – truly one of our sillier borrowings, in that we've already elegantly appropriated the word once, as 'vanguard', which has been part of the language, both literally, as the foremost section of an army, and figuratively, as any sort of trail-blazer, since

1400. It was not until 1910 or thereabouts, when British and American aspirant artists regarded Paris as the home of the arts and must needs pose in proof that they had rubbed shoulders with Fauvists and Post-Impressionists in Montparnasse, that it was felt necessary to speak of 'the *avant garde*, my dear'. The words still have such unfortunate connotations of weak wrists and pretension.

**Avant la lettre** – 'before the letter' or 'before the word existed', so, when people start to make absurd comparisons of the 'Wagner was the Puccini of music' type, they chuck this in to justify anachronism as well as gibberish. 'Rimbaud was a gay biker …,' for example, or 'Lewis Carroll was a rampant paedophile avant la lettre'.

**Avoirdupois** – often used just to mean weights and measures, and often pronounced 'avverdoopers', it is in fact a specific system of weights based on 16oz or 7,000 grains to the lb, and, as might be expected of something evolved over centuries, a mighty fine system it is too. Various foolish bureaucrats have attempted not merely to propose a system founded upon a *kilo* (a platinum cylinder of arbitrary weight kept in Paris) but, on finding it a nigh universal failure with consumers, to enforce it by abuse of 'democratically' afforded powers. The word is not strictly French, but has been part of English since 1656 – *aveir* meaning goods, *de*, of, and *peis* weight.

***Badinage*** – playful conversation, jocular banter, from the verb badiner, to joke or trick. The noun *badine* means a flexible stick or switch, and in France they catch wild ducks by covering a boat with switches in which the ducks seek protection, only to find themselves trapped like a person in a quizzical conversation, shot, plucked, cooked and, worst of all, referred to as fish so that devout Catholics can eat them on Fridays. Whether this is also why *badin* also means 'a fool' in Provençal slang, I am unable to discover, but surely this latter is a more likely immediate source of our word.

**Bagatelle** – an irritating word, because it has an unshakeable herald in the form of 'a mere', and is rarely seen without this prefix. A *bagatelle* is a trifle, a thing of no importance, and has been used to denote such an airy nothing in English since 1637. Although the word comes to us from the French, it originated in Italian, where *baca* means 'berry' in certain dialects. So a *bacatella* is a little or trivial berry or, perhaps, pearl (most such words had technical uses on their introduction, and no doubt a jeweller distinguished between real pearls and *bacatelle*, at which he would have sneered).

As for the popular boardgame 'Bagatelle', the precursor of pinball, it appears to be British in origin and is a modification and miniaturization of billiards for playing in small places such as the snugs or tap-rooms of inns. The game was originally played with nine billiard balls and a cue rather than a spring flipper, a feature introduced only when Bagatelle became a nursery pastime. Between 1770 and 1850, Bagatelle was as popular as billiards throughout Britain. My only suggestion as to the origin of its name is that *bagot* meant a gunstick or drumstick, and that the boardgame may be called after the small cue used – the diminutive suggested, of course, by the existing word.

**Baguette** – a 'French stick' loaf of bread. What could be more archetypally French than the long, thin loaf beneath the onion-seller's arm? Well, lots of things. The word *baguette* has been used of bread only since the 1950s, and the thing itself has existed only since the 1920s. Legend has tried to push the origins of the French loaf further back, maintaining that Napoleon ordered its manufacture so that his soldiers could carry the loaves down their trouser-legs rather than lugging around the *boules* or round loaves which gave the traditional *boulanger* his name. This is hogwash (though imagine the effect on the Grenadier Guards if the Imperial Guard had had a couple of *boules* apiece in their pants).

The *baguette* is the equivalent of our mechanically raised sliced 'bread', a product of bureaucratic intervention in the baker's noble art. The First World War had created a shortage of manpower for the production of France's innumerable traditional sourdough breads, and, in 1920, some vile little jobsworths (whose children were no doubt pillars of Vichy and grandchildren of EU Commissioners) passed a law prohibiting bakers from working before 4 a.m. They were therefore forbidden to take the extra time required for real bread, even had they wished to. They therefore turned to a loaf that could be prepared and baked in short order. No matter that it was stale within hours of baking. This merely meant that customers must return more frequently. Customers with lazy palates and jaws also liked the fluffy texture and sweet, simple flavour of the new white bread.

The word *baguette* was, until the 1950s, principally used in architectural circles of a staff-shaped ornamental feature – a diminutive of the Latin *bacula*, meaning a stick or staff. In or around 1925, jewellers started cutting precious stones in long, thin, faceted shapes and dubbed these '*baguette*-cut'. It might therefore be supposed that *baguette* is related to bague, meaning 'ring', but the resemblance is purely coincidental, and *bague* is one of the remaining French words to come down from the *langue d'oc*. Anyhow, when the bakers started to mass-produce their batons, they borrowed the word and its glittering associations.

**Bain-marie** – a vessel, pan, tray or custom-made utensil containing hot water, in which other pots or pans are placed to keep warm. Originally, so we are told, a pit of hot sand, and invented by a fourth century Jewish alchemist by name Mary, this is a useful implement for the cooking of custards and mumbled eggs for example, for melting chocolate and for keeping sauces (*béarnaise, béchamel, hollandaise*) etc. warm without letting them separate. It is a pernicious implement when used, as was once standard in bad restaurants (including many expensive ones), to keep cooked vegetables and innumerable sauces slowly stewing and festering, often through two separate sittings and more. In this regard, if in no other, the microwave may be considered progress.

**Ballade** – from Provençal *balada*, a dance. As a poetic form, the *ballade* also began life in Provence as an adaptation of the Italian *canzone di ballo* or dancing song. In the fourteenth century, Froissart wrote great *ballades*, in the fifteenth, Villon. For anyone who has an urge to run one off, the eight-line stanza *ballade* contains three eight-line stanzas and a four-line *envoi*, rhyming a-b-a-b-b-c-b-c/b-c-b-c. The ten-line *ballade* lets a 'd' in as well. Chaucer also favoured a *ballade* *royale*, and who will argue with Chaucer? I feel that the little girl who announced, 'This book tells me more about penguins' than I want to know' might here experience *déjà vu* (*qv*).

**Ballon d'essai** – test balloon, an idea 'floated' past critics to see how it 'flies', the *sine qua non* of all original thinking and progress. The Americans partially translate this succinct and elegant term with their 'floating' etc., but today more generally 'run it up the flagpole', again to see how it flies or, sometimes, to see if anyone salutes it – a curiously anachronistic and inapposite version.

**Ballottine** – a culinary term which shuffled reluctantly forward a few years ago on learning that its time to be abused had come. I have since seen it rendered as 'ballontine', 'ballotine' and even 'balantine', usually for some sort of mousse, *galantine* or pudding. In fact, a *ballottine* is boned, stuffed meat, re-formed into a 'little bale', poached or pot-roast and generally served cold in a glaze, jelly or *chaudfroid* (*qv*). You cannot, therefore – though this does not stop them trying – have a 'ballottine' of foie gras, fish or artichoke purée.

**Banal** – commonplace, tawdry. Nineteenth century, from Middle French *banal*, meaning 'subject to military conscription', which was known in mediaeval France as *ban*, as distinct from a Baron or socman who, under Scutage, might be exempt.

**Banquette** – Pumphrey claims that his entire life in France was made up of delightful *banquettes*, including one which he calls 'Corinne' and, apparently, remembers fondly. I have never encountered a delightful *banquette*, let alone one I felt tempted to name, and therefore cannot imagine the sort of life he describes, because a *banquette* is, of course, an upholstered bench along a wall, usually covered in some material designed to stick to human bodies. Originally, however, the word was used of a raised step running along a trench on which soldiers might sit to relax or stand to fire at the enemy. Diminutive of French *banc*, bench, from Italian *banca* and *banchetta*, bench or shelf.

**Barre** – Pumphrey's suggestion that this is where Somerset persons drink is asinine. He thinks that he is contributing to this book because his nephew esteems his erudition. In fact, the boy told me, 'It'll keep him out of trouble, and I'd like him to leave me his bog oak, silver-mounted chemistry set and his house in the Trossachs.' A *barre* is, of course, a hip-high horizontal bar that supplies support to dancers in practising their frolics and gyrations. Why the word 'bar' would not suffice, I am unsure. Artistic refinement, no doubt. Though, interestingly, our word 'bar', meaning 'a longish, evenly shaped piece of some solid substance, such as wood' or 'a counter where beverages are served', is derived from – or, more correctly, used to be spelled – 'barre' in Middle English, because it comes from the Latin *barra*, meaning 'rod', so it is not really a French word at all.

**Bavarois** – a favourite in modern menu-speak, almost always rendered *bavaroise* and almost invariably applied to a confection (often savoury) which is neither. A *bavarois*, or 'Bavarian cheese' is a chilled custard mould, flavoured ad lib and rendered solid by the addition of whipped cream and gelatin. A *bavaroise* is hot, milky tea thickened with beaten egg-yolk and flavoured with liqueur.

**Bayou** – a marshy outlet of a lake or river. The southern United States, and especially lovely Louisiana, are webbed with bayous. This is not, strictly, a French

– or, at least, a French-from-France – word, but a Choctaw term adopted into Louisiana French. In Texas, it means 'a channel to prevent flooding'.

**Beau idéal** – Pumphrey sincerely believed this to mean 'the sort of perfect butterfly which only a good valet could tie,' and I suppose that, to certain people, it might mean just that, in that the *beau idéal* is the ideal of beauty, the Platonic type, the object of usually vain aspiration compared with which all reality is imperfect. A truly dreadful notion, calculated to cause *angoisse* (*qv*) and pointless discontent.

**Beignets** – deep-fried fritters.

**Belle Époque, la** – the 'beautiful era', a nostalgic appellation for a period of France's history which began in the *fin de siècle* at the end of the nineteenth century and extended until the outbreak of the First World War. France is peculiarly fortunate in that a host of clichés, most of them inapposite, overlay the reality. So, while history tells of bloody revolution, Napoleonic attempts to dominate the world, collaboration, over-roast British lamb and bureaucracy as a weapon of mass destruction, cliché tells of the can-can, broad boulevards, Montparnasse cafés, fine food, struggling artists and *oh là là*. All these images come from *la Belle Époque*, in large measure because, with France for once at peace with the world, it became the art-school, strip-joint, refuge for lovers and gap-year student's first destination for the late Victorian and Edwardian British, who tended to maintain outward propriety at home. Art was slight and innovative (Impressionism, Art Nouveau), fashion frippery and daring (Worth, Poiret), music mostly written for the *salon*, so exotic, risqué and accessible. France had bumped off its creative aristocrats, and young artists rushed to fill the vacuum with eccentricity – poet Gérard de Nerval used to walk his lobster on a pale blue lead in the Bois de Boulogne, while Théophile Dondey (who anagrammatised his name to Philotée O'Neddy because he wanted to seem Irish) went to bed with his glasses on, claiming that he was too short-sighted to see his dreams – sexual liberalism and conversation and writings explicitly intended to *épater les bourgeois* (*qqv*). And the bourgeois, of course, loved it.

All the classic images of Paris (not, be it noted, of the rest of France) with the exception of the baguette (*qv*) on a bicycle date from this period. *Gigi* (the book was 1944, the film 1958. Colette's *Claudine* novels are pre-Great War, and she continued to turn out *Belle Époque* tales for the rest of her life), *La Bohème* (1896, drawing on Murger's stories from 1840s), *An American in Paris* (1951, but drawing heavily upon *Belle Époque* cliché), the supremacy of French cuisine (Escoffier became head chef at the London Savoy in 1890 and founded the Carlton nine years later) and the whole British notion of 'French' as deliciously naughty, all are bids to continue *la Belle Époque*. The phrase is now used nostalgically of just about any perceived idyllic, prelapsarian period.

**Belles lettres** – 'fine letters', or any writings of a purely literary nature, such as essays. Generally used as a useful sort of catch-all genre. Where fiction, verse, pornography, natural history etc. are not applicable, it must be *belles lettres*.

**Bête noire** – Pumphrey maintains that this is Creole for 'splendid cheps like Viv Richards and thet Brian Lara'. He is very wrong. Almost always, it appears.

*Bête noire* means 'enemy, bugbear, pet aversion'. Literally, of course, it means 'black beast', but I am unable to discover to precisely what beast it refers. There is the black dog of depression who is also manifest as the 'shuck' of countless English legends and ghost stories. There are any number of bogies which appear in the form of black – presumably because invisible in darkness – creatures. And then, rather more practically and prosaically, there are our own 'black sheep' – undesirable oddballs of less value than their fellows. Brewer opts for this definition: 'The thorn in the side, the bitter in the cup, the spoke in the wheel, the black sheep, the object of aversion. A black sheep has always been considered an eyesore in a flock, and its wool is really less valuable. In times of superstition it was looked on as bearing the devil's mark.' The black sheep enjoyed this unenviable reputation because, of course, its wool was less easy to dye in fashionable colours than that of its white brethren.

**Bibelot** – a trinket or small *objet d'art*. Apparently from an infantile or drunken burbling of the word *bel*, beautiful. So 'an ickew wickew booful fingy'.

**Bidet** – a curious item of bathroom furniture, being a fountain intended to wash the nethers of those rash enough to sit astride it. Some deem this proof of French cleanliness. Others (Pumphrey is vociferous among them, but then he initially maintained that this was an anniversary, shortly before D-day. He has had some black coffee since) believe that it is merely an excuse not to take a bath while leaving the sex organs clean enough to be serviceable, a matter of great importance to our Gallic friends. I have no opinions whatsoever on this matter.

The word *bidet* means 'pony', and is derived in turn from an old French word, *bider*, meaning 'to trot'. Apropos of nothing, it is astonishing how many of our more *recherché* borrowings into English have such mundane, farmyard or veterinary origins. So, for example, we wash astride a pony, dress in our sulking rooms (see *boudoir*) while partaking of a little tea from the finest sow's vulva (yes, that really is the origin of 'porcelain') and then head off to see an improving goat-song (the original meaning of the word 'tragedy').

## Bien coiffée, bien chaussée, bien gantée

– well coiffed, well shod and well gloved, commonly regarded as the essential prerequisites of *chic* in female dress, and in truth far more important than the expensive frock or suit.

**Bien élevé/élevée** – 'well raised' or, as we would say, 'well brought up', well mannered. An example of another variety of borrowing from the French – the *pas devant les enfants* class. I can only assume that French was used here, as so frequently elsewhere, in a mistaken attempt to prevent children and servants from understanding, and that the phrase was therefore commonly used in the negative – 'He's not exactly *bien élevé* …'

**Bien pensant** – 'right-thinking' – a truly despicable, totalitarian term if used literally, and therefore, in English, almost exclusively used ironically of those who, rather than thinking, espouse *idées reçues* (*qv*) and tofu.

**Bijou** – means, of course, 'jewel' or 'gem', and descends to us from the Breton *bizou*, a finger-ring, in turn from *biz*, a finger. Now, I cannot entirely approve of Pumphrey's insistence on sending the charming man from Nott, Frank and Witless or whatever round to the back door on the grounds that he is 'a bloody tradesman', but, given that certain of that sorry business's representatives borrowed this word from the French and without irony used it as an adjective for various properties denoting 'small, cramped and probably malodorous' gives me some sympathy with Pumphrey's stand. Today, at least by educated people, the word is exclusively used with lashings of irony, and often deliberate inappositeness, as in: 'The Queen has that *bijou* little des res at Windsor.'

**Billet doux** – a love letter or note, *not*, as Pumphrey states, 'a nice pad'. *Billet* is 'chit' (a diminutive of *bille*, meaning list or account in old Anglo-French since mediaeval times, and related to our 'bill' and the Papal 'bull'), and *doux*, of course, means 'sweet, gentle'. The phrase has generally retained its diminutive sense, a love letter being a serious composition while a *billet doux* is more likely to be found tucked into or pinned to something or other. Pumphrey's military 'billet' was originally the chit presented by a soldier for his designated board and lodging, and has since been transferred to the lodgings as 'a cushy (Anglo-Indian – Hindi *khush*, healthy, luxurious) billet'.

**Bisque** – God knows. *Bisque* is variously a handicap given to inferior players of croquet, a beigeish colour and a thickish soup. Its origins in all contexts are lost, but our best guesses are as follows: *bis* is, of course, 'twice', and the *bisque* in croquet is an extra shot. One bold Belgian croquet fan even goes so far as to suggest that the *que* is a Flemish diminutive *ke*, but where the Flemish come into the 150-year history of croquet, we are uncertain. As for the colour, this seems to be a characteristic bit of culinary and designer preciousness. A biscuit, known to our American cousins as 'a cookie', is so called because it is (or was) twice-cooked (*bis* – twice, *coctus* – cooked), and, as 'bisket', has been part of the English language since the fifteenth century. Then in the nineteenth century, cooks decided that 'bisket' was not fancy enough and introduced French spelling. In the words of the *OED*, 'the current "biscuit" is a senseless adoption of the modern French spelling without the French pronunciation.'

So far, so predictable. In pottery, 'biscuit' was a term quite reasonably applied to porcelain and pottery which was first fired at one temperature, then glazed or decorated and baked at a higher. In the intermediate stage, before glazing, it was 'biscuit-ware'. This has a beigeish, brownish hue, and the word came to be used to describe the colour. Then along comes some interior designer who shudders from so mundane and domestic a word and decides that *bisque* is suitably *recherché* and *chic*.

As for the soup, the word has existed (as 'bisk') in English since 1647. It is thought to be derived from a dialect French word for a sour soup from the Vendée area around the Bay of Biscay. Originally, this seems to have been a pigeon soup, but *bisque* is now used for soups of lobsters, prawns or crayfish with no properties to distinguish them from any other soups.

**Bistro, bistrot** – a word from Parisian *argot* of very obscure etymology. A wine shop-cum-small restaurant. Usually associated in the English-speaking world with cafés where you can obtain *croque-monsieurs* and French onion soup while reading the newspaper and even, almost unthinkably, chatting with relative strangers. A most civilised contribution, therefore, to the joy of nations. Inevitably, restaurateurs, owners of catering chains and even, Gawd help us, 'chefs', recognising that rapid turnover of diners, informal atmosphere and largely pre-prepared fare make for high profit-margins, have hijacked this notion, and there is an entire genre of 'bistro food'.

In that this is generally preferable to fast food or

dishes requiring skill but executed by those devoid of it, this is moderately good news, not least because *bistros* wish to attract the custom of females, and there is a mistaken assumption that, while men like puddings and chips, women favour salads and poached fish. When, however, a restaurant purporting to be a *bistro* is, in fact, a snotty restaurant charging exorbitant prices for snacks, or, still worse, when a chef decides to place his own mark upon *bistro* food by turning a *croque-monsieur* into 'twin tranches of lightly toasted rustic wholemeal bread with Bayonne ham and a sauce Mornay with seed mustard and capers' or some such, you have cause to weep and to get violently drunk. In the pub next door.

**Blanquette** – stew. Made with white stock.

**Blasé/e** – bored, surfeited with life's pleasures. A most unattractive pose, much affected by infantile adolescents and Englishmen abroad who cannot afford pleasures so affect to despise them. From *blaser*, to satiate.

**Bleu, au** – slip a newly caught trout or other fish (eviscerated through its gills) into plain salt water or *court bouillon* and poach, and lo! you have cooked it *au bleu*. So called because the vinegar with which the fish is first sprinkled turns the slime on the skin a delicate, pearlescent shade of blue.

**Blond, blonde** – fair, light in colour. This has been part of the language since the fifteenth century, and really the only reason for including it here is that it still follows French rules, becoming 'blonde' when descriptive of a female. It has existed as a noun only since 1822.

**Bon appétit** – good appetite. A curious and somewhat gratuitous phrase used to encourage diners, whose appetites, it can generally be assumed, are adequate, which is why they are sitting with knife and fork raised in the first place. Along the lines of the theatrical 'break a leg', which means 'good luck!' though the latter phrase is prohibited, *bon appétit* actually means, 'I hope that you will enjoy, or at least consume without complaint, this Shergarburger or plateful of Gobbets in Stuff.'

**Bonhomie** – friendliness, affability, geniality.

> *'Why, what's the matter?" "Nothing Pooh Bear, nothing. We can't all, and some of us don't. That's*

*all there is to it""Can't all what?" said Pooh, rubbing his nose."Gaiety. Song-and-dance. Here we go round the mulberry bush.""Oh!" said Pooh. He thought for a long time, and then asked, "What mulberry bush is that?" "Bon-hommy," went on Eeyore gloomily. "French word meaning bonhommy," he explained. "I'm not complaining, but There It Is.'"*

Eeyore's definition in *Winnie-the-Pooh* is pretty sound. The word is taken from *bonhomme* or 'good-natured (little) man', the sort of person who makes you wonder if, after all, you want to go to heaven where, it is said, *bonhommes* abound.

**Bon mot** – a witticism, a clever or memorable turn of phrase. *Bon* is good. *Mot* is word, or, in this context, perhaps a little nearer to '*motto*', ingeniously taken from the Italian 'motto' – a saying, from, in turn, Latin *muttire* – to murmur or utter, or *muttum*, a grunt or word.

**Bonne femme** – good wife. In cookery, either a sorrel soup or (*à la*) method of cooking fish in the oven with lots of butter, mushrooms and parsley and a gout of white wine. The liquor is then boiled down and used to glaze the fish. Also, sometimes, though incomprehensibly, a name afforded by the ignorant to a vinous white sauce when poured over fish.

**Boudins** – one of the great triumphs of the *charcutier's* (*qv*) art, a sausage because enclosed in intestine, a pudding because poached. The *boudin blanc* is the subtlest and loveliest of its tribe. Lean pork, chicken or rabbit, onions or leeks and fat, all finely minced, mixed with eggs and cream, lightly spiced and injected into an intestine, the *boudin* is lowered into simmering water, gently cooked, gently drained, then, when thoroughly dried, brushed with clarified butter and grilled or fried.

I cannot understand why this marvel is not served in every *bistro* or *brasserie* worthy of the name and, indeed, since it is so easily made at home, at domestic dinner parties. The *boudin noir*, alas, cannot so readily be made in a domestic kitchen, since its principal ingredients are fresh blood and diced fat. The fillings for both these delights can be the subject of imaginative experiment. I have incorporated sliced sweetbreads, oysters, mushrooms, laver etc. in *boudins blancs* with some success.

The *boudin* of the Cajun kitchen, though delicious, is a coarser confection, making use of pork liver and rice as well as the trimmings from the pig. The English versions are also generally too stuffed with barley, flour and rusk to bear comparison with the real thing. *Boudins* and puddings seem to have coexisted for many centuries, and to have developed along much the same lines. English puddings – mixed cereals, meat and sometimes fruit, boiled or steamed – are recorded in the thirteenth century and are amongst the lost treasures of international cuisine. British so-called chefs drool over their gnocchi, pasta, *saucisses* and *saucissons*, dim sum and the like, but rarely pause to reflect that we had a hugely sophisticated and diverse range of healthy, economical puddings and sausages, sweet and savoury, at first unrecorded, then forgotten as Britain acquired incomparable wealth and took up wasteful roasting instead. Oh, and the word in both languages is said to come to us from the Latin *botellus*, a small sausage. I rather doubt it. We have the Old English *puduc*, a pustule or wen, and Low German *puddig*, bloated, thick (is there a word as wonderful as 'thick'?).

**Boudoir** – a lady's sitting or dressing room, often today wrongly used to denote a bedroom. In fact, a *boudoir*, derived from the French *bouder* – to pout or sulk – means a 'sulking room', a place where a woman may, and therefore quite reasonably does, engage in prolonged emotional blackmail in considerable comfort. In common English usage since 1777.

**Bouffant** – *bouffer* is (onomatopoeically) to puff or blow out, to puff up, so *bouffant* is puffing or swelling, as in skirts, sleeves, soufflés or extravagant hairdos.

**Bouillabaisse** – is *not* a thick fish soup but a rapid method of preparing motley spanking fresh fish with a little oily broth, to be eaten with croûtons. Imagine that you are a Marseillais fisherman with an exigent spouse. You have sold the best of your catch and have a random selection of fish left when a large number of cousins by marriage turn up, expecting, of course, to be fed. There is just one fire and one pot above it, and, being in Provence, *la bonne femme* has already flung in the staples of olive oil, onions, garlic and tomatoes. In goes some saffron, then the firmer-fleshed fish, chopped, then enough water to cover and boil them. Finally, in go the softer fish which require mere minutes to be cooked. The water, which is reduced rapidly at high heat – do you want neighbours saying that you serve just fish boiled in water? – proves a rather delicious, oily broth. It is this last feature which gives the dish its name. *Bouillir* is to boil, and *abaisser* to reduce.

As with most rough and ready dishes, this sometimes works sublimely and sometimes – well – not particularly. This will depend upon a host of factors, among which the quality, variety and freshness of the fish are paramount. This is why *bouillabaisse* has taken on an almost mythic quality. It is not really restaurant food, and the odds against your being in the right place (hard by the sea) at the right time (when the mixture of newly caught fish is good, the diners sufficiently plentiful and poised to eat and the fire stoked) are akin to those against, say, winning the National Lottery or getting through to a responsive human being when calling your bank.

**Bouillon** – stock. From *bouillir*, as above. In English from 1725.

**Bouillon cube** – expensive stock concentrate, generally distinguished by an overwhelming taste of Marmite (Vegemite).

**Boulevard, boulevardier** – a boulevard is a broad street or avenue. The term was first used as such in English by the great Horry Walpole in 1769. Oddly enough, the origin is the Middle Dutch *bolwerc*, the same source as for our far more static and burly 'bulwark', and the word denoted a walkway along a rampart. Of course, shops perched along the city walls and a sense of openness afforded by nothing but a vertiginous drop on either side may have suggested the new meaning, though it has more plausibly been suggested that wide public walks built on the site of demolished city walls, thus creating wide avenues around otherwise cramped towns, may have suggested this adaptation. It was the French, however, who defined the boulevard as now we know it, and, of course, it was during *la Belle Époque* (*qv*) that they did so, with Baron Haussmann and his fellows ripping down the dangerous, dirty old Paris and constructing broad boulevard after boulevard – Strasbourg, Sebastopol, St Germain, Haussmann itself and many others. One of the principal reasons for their breadth was actually to prevent or, at least, impede, the building of barricades by rioters, but it is better to forget that …

A *boulevardier* is one who strolls along boulevards, a man about town.

**Bouquet** – a bunch of flowers, a nosegay. An eighteenth-century borrowing, from the same source as our 'bosky' and 'bush'. A good wine may need no bush (an expression which is derived from wine merchants' habit of festooning their stalls with ivy to identify themselves and attract custom) but it surely profits from a 'little wood' (French *bois*, Latin *boscus*) or bouquet – a poetic extension of the floral meaning.

**Bouquet garni** – small sheaf or faggot of aromatic herbs, usually thyme, parsley and bay, routinely added to stews, stocks and *courts bouillons*. When the resultant broth is to be cooked for more than an hour, this is intended to reassure the cook, since the herbs' virtues (with the exception of the bay) are all but gone by the time that the food is ready.

**Bourgeois, bourgeoise** – generally a disparaging term for a person of the moneyed middle classes, assumed to be censorious, unimaginative, materialistic and fat. Originally, a *bourgeois* was a burgher or burgess – a shopkeeper or other trader operating in a walled town or 'burgh'. Subsequently (sixteenth century), simply a member of the middle classes in general. The feudal distinction, which saw the gentry and peasantry linked by enduring bonds to the land and by expertise in the arts of venery and war while the bourgeoisie, although useful for loans, were dependent upon these for their protection, endures to this day, and was widely preached by the artists and young gentry of *la Belle Époque*, who thought it their duty '*épater* (to startle) *les bourgeois*'.

**Bourgeoise, à la** – braised, usually with chopped carrots, bacon and onion, but also a fancy way of saying 'old-fashioned, middle-class style'.

**Brasserie** – as a *bistro* is to wine, so a *brasserie* is to beer, and, in mediaeval times, it seems that the *brasserie* was the nearest thing to our taverns, in that beer was both made and served there (*brasser* is to mix, mash or brew) and food soon served to accompany it.

It is thought that the *brasserie* came to France from Germany via the long-disputed territory of Alsace. Today, a *brasserie* is indistinguishable from a *bistro*, although there have been rather grander and more pretentious *brasseries*.

**Brassière (bra)** – an article of female apparel, designed to hold the breasts in check and to support them. In French, the word means a baby's vest, and the bosom-holder is known as a *soutien-gorge*, just as, in Dutch, it is called a *bustenhouder*, in German a *bustenhalter*, in Norwegian, a *bysteholder* and, in Portuguese, a *porta-scios*. Brassière is first recorded in a Canadian advertisement of 1911, and in the US Index of Patents for the year 1910 (published in 1911). It is derived from an obsolete (seventeenth-century) French word meaning 'bodice' from the Old French *bracière*, or 'arm protector'.

Although women have worn breast-restraints since ancient Greece, they do not seem to have been designed to enhance and draw attention to these delightful appurtenances but rather to treat them as inconvenient necessities to be confined for ease of movement. One Henry Lesher patented a bra-like piece of armour stated to stress the 'symmetrical rotundity' of breasts in 1859, but it was thirty years later that Herminie Cadolle of France invented the first two-piece undergarment, a confection called *le bien-être* (the well-being). By 1905, the upper half was being sold separately as a *soutien-gorge* ('sustain' or 'hold up' and *gorge*, meaning 'throat', a euphemism for *sein* or breast). The Canadians, therefore, claim priority in the use of the word brassière.

**Bric-à-brac** – trinkets, bits and bobs. From a French nonsense phrase, *à bric et à brac*, meaning 'any old way, hotchpotch, randomly'.

**Bricoleur, bricolage** – a *bricoleur* is a handyman or jack-of-all-trades. *Bricolage* is the construction, repair or adaptation of something with whatever materials happen to be lying around, a haphazard or opportunistic assemblage. Originally from Italian *bricola*, a catapult designed, like a blunderbuss, to fire random stones, bolts etc.

**Brioche** – the king of breads – or is that 'cakes'? Certainly those who translated Marie Antoinette's words, *'Qu'ils mangent de la brioche,'* preferred the latter, and that preference may have owed as much to English confusion as to political prejudice. Yeast-leavened, close-textured and buttery on the tongue but not the fingers, *brioche* shares the nature and the best qualities of both. As good stuffed with oysters or other savoury fillings or as the vector for *foie gras*, as toasted the following day with icing sugar or jam.

**Brochure** – eighteenth century, a pamphlet, from *brocher*, to prick, because a brochure was stitched together.

**Bureau** – a drop-front desk with drawers, whence an office, usually performing a public function. From *burel*, a coarse woollen cloth, presumably used to cover the surfaces of bureaux. A further indication of the appearance of the original, seventeenth-century *bureaux* lies in the fact that *burel* appears to be derived from the Latin *burrus*, red. So 'bureaucracy', the rule of the desk or office, is red tape on red wool.

***Cab*** – what? Well, maybe it shouldn't really be here, but it is derived from *cabriolet* – a very light, two-wheeled, one-horse chaise – a sort of horse-drawn rickshaw – unsuitable for carrying luggage but ideal for rapid trips about town, and therefore the vehicle of choice on the introduction of the *taximètre* or vehicle for hire. It was probably the bounciness of the *cabriolet* which caused its users to give it this name, which is derived from *capriole*, a goat-like leap (from the Latin *caper*, goat) which gives us the word 'caper' and *haute école* equestrianism the name *capriole* for a totally pointless vertical leap, with kick, practised by their mounts.

**Cabaret** – a restaurant or café with entertainment. From French via Old French, Walloon and Dutch *cambret* or *camberet*, little room or chamber. So an intimate place of conviviality or entertainment and so, at last, the entertainment itself.

**Cabochon** – a mound-like cut of gemstone, unfaceted. Star-sapphires and semi-precious stones are generally *cabochon*, diamonds never. From *caboche*, a diminutive in turn of Latin *caput*, head, precisely the same origin as our word 'cabbage'.

**Cache** – hiding place, or everything therein secreted, from *cacher*, to hide. First borrowed from French by North Americans in the eighteenth century. A whole host of suburban euphemistic *cache* words follow on this, so **cache-pot** – a larger, ornamental pot to conceal the fact that flowers are growing in lowly, functional flowerpots and, *horribile dictu*, earth; **cache-mari** – a bunch of flowers or other ornamental table centrepiece, designed to hide spouses from one another; and **cache-sexe** – a covering for the genitals (Pumphrey for some extraordinary reason believed that this meant 'love'. He is a strange man). It is not enough, however, for our linguistic Pooters to hide such gross things, they must also shroud their purpose in anodyne and whimsical French.

**Cachet** – the word *cacher*, as above, had an earlier meaning of 'to press or crowd together'. A *cachet*, therefore, was a seal, pressed on a letter or official document to render it private, and a *lettre de cachet* a communication under seal from the monarch or nobles. 'Cachet', then, has come to mean a distinctive mark or quality indicative of status.

**Cachou** – all but obsolete, a highly scented lozenge or sweet intended to sweeten breath. From seventeenth-century French, from Portuguese *cachu*, from Malay *kacu*.

**Caddy, caddie, cadet** – all essentially the same words, from French *cadet*, essentially, like 'cabbage' and 'cabochon' a diminutive of Latin *caput*, 'head' or, in this case, 'chief'. So a little chief, a minor member or junior branch of a chiefly family, therefore a junior officer or *aide de camp* (*qv*) and so, by the eighteenth century, a student at a military academy. Or, for that matter, a helper and bearer at golf. Or tea-making.

**Cadre** – the central core of a larger organisation of people. Interestingly, from a source which means the opposite, because *cadre* in French means 'frame' – as for a picture – from the Italian *cuadro*, a frame or square (shape).

**Café** – coffee and hence coffee shop, though nowadays more usually associated with mugs of deep tan tea, bacon sandwiches and sausages last seen in *Health and Efficiency* magazine than with fine coffee (from thirteenth-century Arabic *qahwah*) and good conversation.

**Cagoule** – a hooded waterproof garment, often mysteriously rendered (in pseudo-Inuit or something) 'kagoul' or 'kagoule', though in fact simply the French version of our 'cowl', from the Latin *cuculla*, a monk's hood.

**Camaraderie** – wholly unnecessary mid-nineteenth-century borrowing for 'comradeship'. Both words come from Latin *camera*, a room, so a 'comrade' or *camarade* is, in effect, a room-mate.

**Camisole** – a woman's undergarment or under-bodice, formerly a man's short jacket. Literally, of course, a little *camisia* (Latin for shirt), descending to modern French in the word *chemise*. English vagrant cant also has 'commission' or 'mish' for shirt for the same reasons.

**Canapé** – a small amount of foodstuff on a vector, usually a *croûton* (*qv*) or biscuit (No, damn it. Bisket.) Both this word and 'canopy' – a suspended covering – come from the Greek for mosquito, *konops* (while we are at it, the word *oestrus*, meaning the cycle of sexual urges in the female, comes not from a cognate of 'Easter' but from *oistros*, the Greek for a gadfly, so *oestrus* nips at you and makes you mad or skittish) and its derivative *konopeion*, a bed with a mosquito net. So, in English, this root grew up to be a protective or ornamental covering for a bed or seat, while, in French, it became a couch itself. So the French word for 'couch' was imported to serve for a food on a 'bed'.

**Canard** – is, of course, a duck, and is onomatopoeic, coming from *caner*, to quack. In English, however, the word denotes a false report or rumour, a sense which also exists in modern French. It is believed that this curious association is derived from a common French expression dating from the sixteenth century, *vendre un canard à moitié*, or 'to sell half a duck', which, of course (we are here talking about the living creature, not the crispy, juicy, roasted variety) is impossible, and so means to con or to 'sell a pup'. This last expression almost certainly comes from the same source as 'a pig in a poke' and 'let the cat out of the bag'. It was once common practice to sell a piglet in a bag or 'poke' – hence our 'pocket' – and let the buyer take a chance on its quality, plumpness and fitness. Of course, a crook might slip a plump pup or a cat into the poke and would hope that the cat was not let out of the bag and that the buyer did not discover that he had been sold a pup until he was a good distance away.

**Cap à pie** – From Old French, 'head to foot'. So 'fully armed'.

**Caprice** – a whim or whimsicality. Originally, this came from the Italian *capriccio* from *capo*, head, and *riccio*, urchin or hedgehog, so 'hair standing up like quills', and the word meant 'horror', a fact which might usefully be noted by those who call their unfortunate daughters 'Caprice' in emulation of some gaunt mannequin or other. In the seventeenth century, this modulated to mean a sudden change of mood.

**Carousel** – a roundabout, whether of the fairground variety or that which ingeniously brings you other people's luggage while carefully sifting out and battering your own. From a chivalric term for jousting practice, derived from French *carrousel*, a joust, from Italian *carosello*, a mounted joust of some variety or other.

**Carte blanche** – total licence. Literally 'blank paper', the implication being that a person given such a thing may fill it in at will.

**Cartel** – a word with mildly surprising origins. Originally, a *cartel* in French was a little card or note containing a challenge to battle or a duel. In the nineteenth century, this became an agreement made between combatants or people at odds, later extended to mean an agreement or partial pact between rivals in order to fix prices etc. and thereby so obscene a concept that we would expect a French euphemism for the dirty French word.

**Cassette** – a little case or, in French, *case* or *caisse*, so a casket and/or little case for a spool of film or recording tape.

**Catalogue raisonné** – a 'reasoned catalogue' – that is, an ordered catalogue of an artist's work, for example, with explanations, chronology and descriptions. Generally, this term is used for that which 'catalogue' by definition should describe – the totality of that listed. The Greek prefix *kata* means 'total' or 'complete', where *logein*, of course, is to speak, record or log.

**Cause célèbre** – *cause* was initially merely an alternative for *chose* – a matter or thing. A *cause célèbre* is therefore just a famous matter or affair, generally a legal case or campaign of general public interest.

**Cerise** – cherry, from Greek *kerasia*, a cherry tree. This springs from a Middle Eastern source, because the cherry is not native to Europe. So too the colour cherry-pink, which is a much prettier coupling of words but not so *recherché*-sounding.

**C'est la vie** – when I asked Pumphrey about this, he started to sing 'A Life on the Ocean Wave' and babbled of rum, sodomy and the lash. Again, miles from the mark. This means, of course, 'That's life', as in the Frank Sinatra song about puppets and paupers and pirates and poets. A general expression of resignation, thought to be consoling, and perhaps better in French because it invariably accompanies a peculiarly Gallic shrug.

**Céviche (séviche)** – a South American and Polynesian method of preparing raw fish by marinating it in lemon or lime juice rather than cooking it by heat. If you add a little sugar and black pepper, the result is often delicious, *unlike* Kosykwik's Olde Sea Dogge Battered Mariners' Codpieces, which are thought by some sufficient sustenance for the exacting work of compiling a dictionary …

**Chacun à son goût** – … talking of which, this is a disgraceful, relativist resignation of responsibility, 'every person to his taste', implying that people have as much right to like pre-prepared battered codpieces or daytime television as we to like pigs' trotters stuffed with sweetbreads or Mozart, which, of course, they have not. Or rather, it is no doubt an excellent thing that they do, because they leave our favourite restaurants and the Highlands of Scotland unscarred by dayglo fleeces, glottal stops and synthesised cheese-and-prawn-flavoured women and crisps, but education brings with it a responsibility to propagate further education and taste. It is all most vexing, but this expression basically means, 'I am too damned craven and shiftless to fight my own corner and that of my culture.' Ha.

**Chagrin** – disgruntled annoyance, resentment or melancholy such as is felt by those who have known real life and are reduced to battered codpieces. Probably from a rather jolly obsolete French word, *chagreiner*, which means to cloud over or become gloomy. '*Plaisir d'amour ne dure qu'un moment*,' says the lovely French ditty all too horribly truly. '*Chagrin d'amour dure toute la vie*.' So why we do it, God alone knows. The link with 'shagreen' – rough, grained leather or sharkskin – implying that 'chagrin' is an itch of some sorts, is very dubious.

**Chaise longue/percée** – ah, the 'hurly burly of the *chaise longue*', usually resulting in serious sciatic problems and sometimes contusions and children, not to mention the *chagrin d'amour* which, as the song so rightly says, lasts a lifetime ... A *chaise longue* is, of course, a long chair, suitable for reclining. A *chaise percée* is a chair with a hole in it or, as we would say, a commode, permitting the user to receive guests, as was Louis XIV's curious wont, 'at stool'.

**Chalet** – a cabin or small house in the Swiss style. The word comes to us from Swiss French, and indicates what we would call a 'bothy' or mountain shelter, but, of course, these in orderly Switzerland resemble cuckoo-clocks, which a British estate agent would no doubt describe as 'bijou chalet-style residences'.

**Chambré** – sometimes Pumphrey can be quite endearing. He actually thought that this word referred to a donkey's field. The shrapnel is still moving, apparently. Of wine, brought to room temperature. A useful, succinct and direct borrowing, taken from, of course, *chambre*, a room, from Latin *camera*.

**Chamois** – a goatlike antelope and the scraps of leather from same, widely used for polishing coach-work etc. and informally known as a 'shammy'. The

PAR AVION chamois and its Pyrenean cousin, the *gamuza*, both derive their names from the late Latin *camox*.

**Champignon** – mushroom or toadstool (the words used to be interchangeable in English). A pointless borrowing. Originally from *champagne*, from the Latin *campania*, meaning level country.

**Champlevé** – a sort of enamelling in which the colours are laid in grooves or panels cut into the metal, so that the *champ*, or field, is *levé*, or higher.

**Chancre** – a painless genital tumour, a sign of syphilis. From, of course, dear old Cancer the Crab.

**Chanson/chanteuse** – er, respectively song and female singer. Heaven knows what the French terms afford which the English ones do not, but there …

**Chaperon/chaperone** – again originally from Latin *caput*, head, so a hood or 'little cape' (or a funny little escutcheon hanging from the browband of a horse), so a person, usually an older woman, charged with preserving the virtue and welfare of a young woman, or, if literary convention serves, more commonly responsible for her losing her virtue whilst maintaining outward propriety. Whether this comes from the garments worn by such women or from their protective function is unclear.

**Charabanc** – pronounced 'sharrabang' in English, a motor coach or horse-drawn coach with ranks of seats facing forward, obviously from *char*, from Latin *carrum*, a wagon (whence also 'chariot' and 'car'), *à bancs* – or 'with benches'.

**Charade** – a guessing game, so a pretence or simulation necessary to such a game. Charades is known as 'the game' to the British upper classes.

**Charcuterie** – the preparation and processing of pork, as sausages, *boudins*, hams, bacon, *andouillettes*, *pâtés* etc.

**Chargé d'affaires** – a person charged with specific affairs or business in a minor state, usually where an ambassador is unsuitable or out of action.

**Chassis** – the frame of a car or other motor vehicle, but formerly that of a mounted gun, and before that (seventeenth century) of a window or, as we would say, 'casement'. From Latin *capsa*, a box or case.

**Château** – commonly rendered 'castle' because the root of the two words is the same – the Latin *castellum*. In fact, of course, an English 'castle' is a fortified bastion, a building whose design is dictated by its defensive function rather than by comfort or whimsy, while the majority of *châteaux* are merely large houses, many of them almost purely whimsical confections of turrets and no more defensive than a cat with a raised tail.

**Chateaubriand** – pointless term for a length of fillet of beef cooked in one piece, rather than sliced in steaks before cooking. More strictly, it should be a dirty great chunk from the centre of the fillet, served with potatoes cut into strips and cooked in butter (*château*) and a *sauce béarnaise*. Named, it seems, after René, Vicomte de Chateaubriand (1768–1848), a French writer and statesman.

**Chatelaine** – in French *châtelaine*, the mistress of a *château* or country house, often applied to boarding-house landladies and the like.

**Chatoyant** – a word which we should use more often, it describes an undulant or shifting shimmering or iridescence, like that of satin underwear in motion, perhaps, or the cat's eyes from which it derives its existence.

**Chaudfroid** – literally 'hot-cold', a dish made with and enclosed by a hot sauce which, generally with the assistance of gelatin or aspic, is served cold, so that the sauce encases or encapsulates the ingredients within. Many a terrine and raised pie is thus essentially a *chaud-froid* dressed up in bacon or pastry.

**Chef (n)** – strictly *chef de cuisine* – a person more or less skilled in the culinary crafts, and therefore engaged to supervise others in the preparation of foods. The status of 'chef' is dependent, like, say, that of a 'king', 'conductor' or 'director', upon an indirect object. You have to be chef over others. A former chef without a kitchen is technically known as 'an unemployed person'. A person who cooks but does not run a full kitchen staff is known as 'a cook'. A person who has no kitchen but who, on the television or the page, tells others how to cook, is known as 'a jammy bastard'. A person referring to himself or herself as 'chef' or wearing a chef's hat without staff or kitchen is referred to as 'a fraud'. No less than a nobleman regards 'a good servant' as the highest accolade to which he can aspire, so the cook wishes only to be referred to as 'a fine cook'. The words 'a good chef' may be applied to a person with knowledge of, but little skill in, cooking, just as an orchestral conductor may be a virtuoso on none of the instruments in his control. **Chef de partie** – as above, but in charge of a department *(partie)* such as sauces, grills etc. and under the control of the chef. It is a brave chef who presumes to include *pâtisserie* among his *parties*.

And, while we are at it... **Sous chef** – under, or, preferably, deputy chef. An aspirant groveller, but generally more megalomaniacal than his master when left in charge. **Commis chef** – primordial, invertebrate life-form with magical properties. Leave knobbly, muddy, brown things in proximity to one such and they are converted into nice, white potatoes. *Commis chefs* feel no pain. Kicking and abusing them is therefore a complete waste of energy. On the other hand, it is generally found to be quite therapeutic. A *commis chef* is so called because of its political 'views' and its inability to spell. Within one month, the lowliest rat in a well-run kitchen is a violent, radical Trotskyite and, naturally, its inferiors follow suit. There is justice, however. Eventually, even *commis* can evolve into chefs. They then adopt the politics and morals of Caligula. Actually *commis* is the past participle of *commettre*, to entrust. Ha!

**Chef d'oeuvre** – chief (or principal) piece of work, so the greatest work in an artist's corpus.

**Chemin de fer** – a railway or, literally, 'road of iron'. Also a version of baccarat or 'twenty-one' much favoured by high-rollers. Irrelevantly, 'baccarat' is descended from the Italian *bacarra*, which means 'zero'. It is said that this in turn was an evolution of an ancient Etruscan ritual, in which the nine gods stood reverently about a blonde virgin, as one certainly would, while she endeavoured to throw an eight or a nine on a nine-sided die. If she managed it, she became a priestess. If she threw a six or a seven, she was excluded from all other sacred functions. Anything lower than six, and she must walk into the sea, and, we assume, not walk back, which is a profligate waste of blonde virgins.

**Chenille** – a thick, velvety cotton cord, formerly used for making bedspreads and trimming lamp-shades, hats and gowns, but now widely used as a knitting yarn in its own right, *chenille* means 'hairy caterpillar', but is derived from the Latin canicula, or 'little dog'.

**Cherchez la femme** – 'seek the woman ...' The implication here is that, wherever there is contention, a woman, or a man's passion for a woman, will be found to be causing or inciting it. Disgracefully sexist. Generally true.

**Chère amie** – bit of cuff or skirt. Literally 'dear female friend'.

**Cheval de bataille** – literally warhorse, used to denote an obsession or, as we would say, a 'hobby-horse'.

**Chevron** – a 'V'-shaped heraldic device or joint in rafters, from *chèvre*, though whether because of the shape of a goat's legs or its horns is unknown.

**Chez** – at the home of. From Latin *casa*, cottage, so, in the dative, at the cottage of …

**Chic** – entered English in the mid-nineteenth century, denoting 'smart, stylish, neat'. The connotations have become many and, for once, render translation impossible. They include a certain sparseness of decoration and cleanliness of line. It also denotes an ethos, an attitude, a totality as distinct from its individual components, so a young lady in a little black dress may be *chic*, but the frock cannot truly be so of itself.

**Chicane/chicanery** – a curious word. *Chicanerie* in Middle French is sophistry or Jesuitical quibbling, a sense retained in modern French, *chicaner*, to quibble. In English from the seventeenth century, however, it has come to mean trickery or subterfuge. Hence, in time, a sharp bend or double bend on a racetrack (a little bit like the English 'Haha', that invisible ditch so called because that is what people invariably said when they found themselves falling in it). A chicane is also a hand dealt in cards without trumps.

**Chi-chi** – gastro-pubs and French euphemisms and frilly bog-roll holders and people who will not eat offal are *chi-chi* or needlessly refined and offensively inoffensive. The word's origins are unknown, but it appears to have become current in both English and French at the turn of the nineteenth to twentieth centuries.

**Chiffon/chiffonier/chiffonnier/chiffonade** – chiffon is a very fine and so diaphanous silk or man-made fabric, and takes its name from *chiffe*, a rag. One likes to think that housemaids would distinguish between a good, serviceable clout and one worn and frayed to a mere *chiffon*, and indeed a *chiffonnier*, in English and French, is a rag-picker or collector of household scraps. A *chiffonier*, however, is a high bureau, because once it was a chest of drawers for scraps of fabric. As for a *chiffonade*, this is the assortment of vegetables cut into strips, or *julienne*, usually as a constituent of soups, and I can only think that, originally, 'take a *chiffonade*' meant 'collect trimmings and peelings' as the rag-picker collects his threadbare scraps …

**Chignon** – lovely word. The nape of the

neck, from Old French *chaignon*, a link in a chain (so, perhaps, the clasp of a necklace or collar?), and so a coil or swirl of hair worn at the back of the neck.

**Chinoiserie** – needless but succinct word for Oriental and, specifically, Chinese furniture, porcelain etc. and the genre imitative of imported Chinese goods which flourished in the eighteenth century.

**Chouette** – there are moments when etymologies appear self-evident though the evidence is sparse. I am convinced that *chouette*, the delightful *argot* word for 'cool', 'nifty', 'keen', 'sweet', owes its existence to a two-way interchange with English. Originally, *chouette* means barn owl or little owl, though the term is widely used in rural areas of France and Canada to denote any small variety of owl. This is surely, given the resemblance to our 'To-whit', a name imitative of the bird's call. It is from the owl's multi-directional vision and swivelling eyes, however, that *chouette*'s other meaning – the player of a game, commonly backgammon, set to play against more than one adversary – surely comes. Now, no one seems to know whence comes the common usage, but I suspect that it is the linguistic equivalent of our wolf-whistle (another to-whit, to-woo) and may be suggested by our own word, 'sweet' or, even, 'ser-weeet!' – that, in other words, the term *chouette* was originally used on its own as an exclamation and only subsequently became an adjective …

**Choux** – a variety of pastry. This occasions justifiable bemusement, because *chou*, of course, means 'cabbage' and is also a familiar and common endearment –'*mon p'tit chou* …'. Although Pumphrey believes that the term '*choux* pastry' is a French phonetic borrowing from English, relating to the resemblance between the texture of Kosykwik's *profiteroles* (*qv*) and his footwear, he is utterly wrong. Little stuffed *friandises* were called *choux* back in the seventeenth century. Yet wherein lies the resemblance between the pastry and a cabbage, and why would anyone refer to a beloved as 'my cabbage'? The usual explanation is that the endearment relates to the pastries – 'my sweetie' or 'honey' – and it is also claimed that the cakes owe their name to the endearment – 'little darlings' or whatever. This seems plausible on both counts, particularly since the word is caressingly euphonious and so ideal for an endearment, but which came first, and how the unattractive vegetable connotations did not overwhelm the appealing associations with sweetmeats, I cannot say.

**Cicatrice** – a scar or the mark of a scar. From Latin *cicatrix*, also a scar.

**Cinéaste** – a silly, prinking word for a cinema enthusiast, now generally replaced by 'film-buff', an American term which purportedly owes its meaning of 'enthusiast' to the colour of the uniform of New York's volunteer firemen, who were desperately keen on their job, or, rather, according to Herbert Asbury (forget the turbid, drooling film. *The Gangs of New York* is still obligatory reading), fiercely competitive over the securing of hydrants, whether the fire raged or no. A 'buff' therefore came to be known as an ardent devotee of just about anything.

**Cinéma vérité** – verisimilitudinous motion pictures. Cinema is itself a French borrowing (*not* so called because Pumphrey used to go to the Brora flea-pit without his mother), taken from cinematograph, the inventors' coining for a projector, from the Greek *kinema* – movement and *graphe* – writing. *Cinéma vérité* or 'cinema truth' is a spurious bid to represent reality 'realistically' by means of film.

**Cinq à sept** – 'five to seven', a most considerate and courteous French institution (and, indeed, English and American, though we do not dare to refer to it) – the visit of a man or a woman to his or her lover (or to a bordello in the case of the indigent or unfortunate) between leaving work and returning to the bosom of the family, and so, less politely, the person so visited. 'She was his *cinq à sept* for two years until his wife died ...' One with a *cinq à sept* is devoted to his family, orderly, rational and courteous, unlike those with more ramshackle and spontaneous arrangements.

**Cire perdu** – 'lost wax', one of the most ancient methods of casting bronze, glass etc., whereby a model is made and spread or otherwise coated with wax. Molten metal or glass is then poured into the mould, displacing the wax which drains out, so creating a perfect replica of the original model.

**Clairvoyant/clairvoyance** – 'clear seeing', a word which means the precise opposite. A clair-voyant gazes into a crystal ball, consults Florence Nightingale or Chief Bear Who Excretes Profusely or some such, and announces, 'It's cloudy, but I seem to see a dark man whose forename begins with "J" and a journey involving wheels, some pain, though I cannot make out the precise cause, and some happiness ...' Clairvoyance occasionally retains its literal meaning in conversation, as in 'he was peculiarly clairvoyant about property prices ...'

**Claque** – a body of people appointed to applaud *pour encourager les autres* (*qv*). From *claquer*, to clap.

**Cliché** – a worn, weary phrase or figure of speech, rendered threadbare by use. From *clicher*, to strike molten lead to obtain a cast, whence the *cliché*, a metal stereotype used in printing (early nineteenth century). Clichés, it should be noted, are usually clichés because once they were expressive and vivid, and, distasteful though Latinate, abstract clichés and truisms may be, few things are so poignant and inelegant as a non-poet desperately skirting standard forms of descriptive expression and attempting to replace them with his own.

**Cloche** – a bell in French, so a bell-glass to cover and contain plants, insects etc., so too a bell-shaped hat.

**Cocotte** – round metal, pyrex or ovenproof earthenware cooking receptacle for steaming, baking or grilling. Apparently from Latin *cucuma*, a cooking vessel. I find this implausible.

**Coif, coiffeur, coiffeuse, coiffure** – a coif is a skullcap, and 'to coif' has been to cover with some sort of cap or cosy since the fifteenth century. Because few ladies ventured forth without headdresses of one form or another and the hair was arranged to fit about such, 'coiffure', meaning 'arrangement of the hair', has existed in English since the seventeenth century. The sense of 'dressing the hair' is a nineteenth-century introduction, possibly because the 'coiffeur', who had formerly made wigs and caps, continued in business when natural hair became fashionable. Certainly we find 'coiffeur' in Thackeray.

**Collage** – bits of paper, fabric etc. glued to a field to make a design. A surprisingly new word, introduced in the twentieth century and derived from the French for gluing, originally from the Greek *kolla*, glue.

**Comédie humaine** – 'the human comedy', so, to cite other clichés, the warp and weft of human existence, all human life, the human condition etc. This term became general when Honoré de Balzac used it, with a nod to Dante's *Divina commedia*, as the overall title of his hugely successful novels of nineteenth-century France.

**Comédienne** – weird. A female comedian. Presumably the French feminine form was adopted because 'comedianess' is ugly, though precisely why and when such gender distinction is necessary at all eludes me. *En passant*, the word 'comedy' comes to us from the Greek *komoidia*, an amusing or diverting spectacle (from *komos*, a carnival or festival, and *aoidos*, singer), but came to mean, by Shakespeare's time, merely a narrative with a happy ending. The current meaning of something designed to make us laugh is far closer to the Greek original.

**Comme ci, comme ça** – 'like this, like that', so 'so-so', 'of variable merit', like the curate's egg. We can see the waggling, outstretched hand, coupled with the shrug, which inevitably accompanies this phrase and renders it all but superfluous.

**Comme il faut** – correctly, 'as it should be', though literally 'as it must be'.

**Commis** – see **Chef**.

**Commissionaire** – originally a person entrusted (as commis) with running errands or conveying messages. In the nineteenth century, this became the familiar uniformed doorman at clubs, restaurants etc., still entrusted with errands such as finding messages, conveying visiting cards etc., though the term's adoption may have owed something to the fact that the role was commonly taken by old soldiers still in possession of His Majesty's commission.

**Commode** – we have two sorts of commode in English. One is the covered *chaise* percée of the sort purchased by the young man of Madrid who went to an auction to bid. It will be recalled that, in that instance, the first thing he 'bode' was an ancient commode which, so the chronicler asserts, went 'poof!' when he lifted the lid. The second variety is a chest of drawers. It is as well not to confuse these. The word is taken from the French *commode* which means 'suitable' as well as 'useful' or 'convenient'. Which sense is here intended it is impossible to say.

**Communard** – a member of a commune, but, from association with the Paris Commune which formed a quasi-government for France for a couple of months in 1871 and, perhaps, with communism, the word has come to mean something like 'a person who would be a member of a commune if only he or she were not too busy preaching communism and attempting to rule the world'.

**Communiqué** – a communication, a bulletin. A jobsworth word, intended to convey the hitherto unsuspected importance of a memo.

**Compagnon de voyage** – a travelling companion. Once, many people such as widows and widowers, young ladies eager to evade unwanted advances and families travelling abroad with young children, had companions, either paid as such travelling *au pair* (*qv*) or simply living with them to provide companionship, conversation and assistance, and a very civilised practice it was too. Today, a woman who decides that she prefers to share her cabin with another woman or a man who offers a young man an opportunity to see the world as his *compagnon de voyage* is at once assumed to be motivated not by reason but by genital stirrings. Such is enlightenment.

**Compote** – compost of fruit, stewed and reduced in syrup. The word *composita* literally means 'things put together', hence also 'composite' and 'compost'.

**Concassé** – roughly chopped or 'broken together' but, in the case of tomatoes, for some extraordinary reason, neatly diced after skin, water and seeds have been removed.

**Concierge** – janitor, warden, steward, originally from, it is thought, Latin *conservus*, fellow-slave. The *concierge* of a block of flats or whatever is generally a foul-tempered, officious individual. The American artist Whistler, on seeing hearty British artists swinging clubs and doing press-ups in their Paris studio, asked, 'Can't you get the *concierge* to do that sort of thing for you?' Alas, in general, one seldom can. Janitor, by the way (from *janua*, a door or archway, and, of course, the god of doors, Janus) is almost certainly the root of the name of that delicious fish, the John Dory, known as a *Saint Pierre* in France because it bears the mark of the prophet's thumb on its shoulder. And St Peter is the gatekeeper or *gianitore*, so … Just thought you'd like to know …

**Concours d'élégance** – very fancy name for a parade of old motor vehicles, judged, as are horses and dogs at shows, regardless of functionality or health but merely on the basis of 'elegance'.

**Confit, confiture** – *confit*, generally of goose (*d'oie*), of duck (*de canard*), or of pork (*de porc*), is a method of preserving meat by cooking and bottling it in its own fat, thus sealing it from the air. This is, incidentally, a very useful method of preservation for sausages, which are best preserved in lard rather than frozen. The same principle is even extended to wine in Sicily, for example, where it is topped with a finger's width of olive oil, but I digress. **Confiture**, while preserving the same sense of – well, preservation – means jam. Both words, and the older *comfit*, generally used for a sweet, come from the Latin *confecta*, made or prepared together.

**Congé** – leave of passage or permission to take a break, improbably said to be from *commeare*, to come and go.

**Connoisseur** – from *connaître*, to know, except that it used to be *connoistre* (the circumflex frequently indicates a missing 's') from Latin, *cognoscere*. So 'a knower', one with expertise or, more commonly, discernment.

**Conservatoire** – an academy of music, dance or other performing arts. Needlessly pretentious borrowing to indicate artistry and so refinement, since we have the words 'academy' and 'conservatory'. A greenhouse is referred to as a 'conservatory' because, like the schools, it is intended to preserve or conserve what might otherwise be threatened.

**Consommé** – a clarified meat, game or fish stock or *bouillon*, from *consommer*, to finish, complete or consummate, so the sense here seems to be of flavours or of essences completely extracted from ingredients and completely pure.

**Conte** – short story, tale, from the same root, of course, as our own 'account', 'recount' and the borrowed *raconteur*, a teller, or reteller, of tales or accounts.

**Contretemps** – a disagreement or row. I came down this morning to see that someone had written 'in favour of sugar-spoons' against this word, which is simply ridiculous. This meaning – the disagreement, not the cutlery preference – is very late. The original meaning – 'against time' or 'offbeat', was used to denote a fencing thrust at a moment when it was not expected or at the same moment as an opponent also thrusts, hence any untimely or unexpected incident, hence, reverting at least in part to the technical sense, a 'clash' between two people.

**Convenance** – agreement, common usage, convenience, from *convenire*, to agree or come together. *A mariage de convenance* therefore means not, delightful as that might be, a marriage of fortuitous amorous synchronisation, but one arranged by mutual agreement or convention, usually in order to preserve or enlarge inheritances.

**Coquette, coquetry, coquettish** – a *coquette* is a flighty, flirtatious floozie, pert and provocative and much given to 'gecking' (a much-needed word from the Gaelic; a 'geck' is 'a wanton toss of the head'), wiggling and other such delicious artistry. She provokes desire without, generally, the least intention of gratifying it. She trifles. Literally, she is deemed 'a little cock', in that she bears herself with the arrogance and the amorous strut of Chanticleer, the ruler of the roost. *Coquet* used to exist for the narcissistic male floozie.

**Cordon bleu** – qualification for young women of gentle or elective Caesarean birth, which demonstrates that they can, almost unaided, prepare a cheese soufflé, a salmon en croûte and a lemon mousse for property developers and bankers seeking wives and for their drug-dealers. Literally 'blue ribbon', because this denoted the highest degree of chivalry under the Bourbon kings, whence the Derby is known as the 'blue ribbon' (or, whimsically, 'riband') of the turf.

**Cordon sanitaire** – 'sanitary ribbon' – originally an area encircling one infected in order to keep germs and infected persons in and those uninfected out (the sense of 'cordon' as a 'surrounding area' dates from the nineteenth century). Nowadays generally used figuratively.

**Corsage** – the word has existed in English since the sixteenth-century, meaning the upper torso or trunk, as in French. The sense of a nosegay pinned to the breast is a twentieth century American innovation, as is the return to French pronunciation in a bid to avoid coarseness.

**Cortège** – a train or procession of people following someone or something. Originally from the Italian *corteggio/corteggiare* – those who attend court and the act of doing so, just as a courtesan was a *corteggiana*, or one who attended court.

**Coterie** – a group or circle of friends or associates. From the same French source as cottage and cotter (*cote* – hut or hovel), a *coterie* was a group of tenants holding land in common from the same landlord. The word 'cottage', by the by, is a Frenchified English invention since adopted into French.

**Coulee/coulée** – a watercourse, the bed of an occasional stream, a Canadian (and so Cajun) borrowing from the French word for a lava flow, from *couler*, to flow, and ultimately from Latin *colare*, to strain, whence 'colander'.

**Coulis** – thin purée, thick soup or sauce with a slow-slipping texture or, more commonly today, sieved mush, purée or compote (*qv*) of fruit. From *coulisser*, to slide (so a portcullis is a sliding door, which is beside the point, or, more accurately, 100 miles as the crow flops from the point, but I'm glad to know it).

**Coup d'état/de foudre/de grâce/de main/de théâtre** – I might as well dispose of Pumphrey's contribution to academe first and foremost. He initially stated that a *coup de grâce* was a lawnmower, but I pointed out that Nicholas Bentley had already made that joke. He then flounced and pouted and insisted that he had, as it happens, eaten a *coup de grâce* at a hippy commune in California in the 1960s. This, or something like it, is very likely to be true, and would explain a lot. He then tetchily wrote down his explanations of *coup d'état* – 'murmur endearments (of Argos staff)', *coup de foudre* – 'murmur endearments (of caterers)' and *coup de grâce* – 'murmur endearments when stoned'.

Anyhow, a *coup* is a blow or stroke, from the Latin *colaphus*, a punch. A *coup d'état* is 'a blow of the state', a revolution or usurpation; a *coup de foudre* is a stroke of lightning, so any Damascene revelation or love at first sight; a *coup de grâce*, the stroke of grace or mercy, the quick, clean blow which brings easeful death to the suffering; a *coup de main* a stroke of the hand, a punch, and so any unforeseen attack; and a *coup de théâtre* a showstopper, a startling development in a drama, and so, confusingly, often a successful performance or an impressive cat pulled out of an otherwise unprepossessing bag.

**Coupe** – a goblet or shallow bowl, so (early twentieth century) a pudding, usually of ice-cream and fruit or *coulis* (*qv*) – so, perhaps, MISTER would-be-comedian Pumphrey, a *coupe de glace* …

**Coupé** – a car with two doors, so called because perceived as 'cut off' (*couper*, to cut), from the French *carrosse coupé*, a cut or shortened carriage with just two seats inside.

**Couture, couturier, couturière, haute couture** – couture is dressmaking, from *cousture* or *costure*, sewing, in turn from Latin *consuere*, to sew together – *suere* gives us 'suture'. Imported in the early twentieth century, the years of Worth and Poiret, when all fashionable frocks came from Paris. In an age of mass production, *haute couture*, formerly a term to distinguish the ornate and innovative from the quotidian (see *école* and *cuisine*), has come to mean clothes hand-made and custom-designed in the *atelier* or studio of the *couturier/couturière*.

**Crème** – a term denoting both cream and custard. Here are a few of the most frequently found: **crème anglaise** (English cream): custard; **crème brûlée**: thick custard, baked in a *bain-marie* and sprinkled with sugar, which is then caramelised under a grill or with a blowtorch until *croquant* (*qv*) *not* invented at Trinity College Cambridge; **crème caramel**: *crème renversée* which has been baked in a bowl lined with liquid caramel; **crème Chantilly**: whipped double cream mixed with sugar and vanilla essence; **crème épaisse** (also **fleurette**): double cream; **crème fraîche**: soured cream; **crème pâtissière**: in essence, a very thick, very sweet *béchamel*, further thickened by the addition of eggs and quite a lot of butter; **crème renversée**: any custard which is turned out after cooking.

**Crème de la crème** – the elite, the best of the best, literally 'cream of the cream'. It is worth pointing out that the scum also rises.

**Crêpe** – pancake, or fabric with a crinkly texture. From Latin *crispus*, *crispa*, curled, whence we derive our own 'crisp'. The fabric appears to have come first, being widely used in late eighteenth-century Britain, whereas the usage referring to pancakes dates from no later than the late nineteenth century.

**Cri de coeur** – cry of, or from, the heart. Self-explanatory in every regard.

**Crime passionnel** – a crime of passion, motivated by sexual jealousy, which was traditionally considered a mitigating if not entirely exonerating circumstance. Why no English cook has ever come up with a cream (or *crème*) *passionnelle* eludes me.

**Crise** – crisis, so **crise de conscience** – crisis of conscience; **crise de nerfs** – attack of the screaming heeby-jeebies etc. …

**Critique** – absurd borrowing, meaning a critical

article, essay or verbally expressed opinion. A person of gentle birth and discernment, on finding himself using this term, will realise that he has betrayed the one and forever lost the other, and will therefore go to the library (by now no doubt converted games console room with hot-tub) and do the decent thing. But hearken and shudder. There are teachers – people entrusted with the care of our impressionable young – who use this term quite openly in front of minors *as a verb*! Some maintain that such people can be treated. For myself, I doubt it. It hurts me to say it, but I seriously believe surgery to be the only answer. When once their tongues and thumbs are removed, they will learn to express themselves by more honest, original and imaginative means, such as cupping their remaining fingers to solicit alms, without having to resort to a precious, complex language which is plainly beyond them.

The priority, of course, is avoidance. Look out for the first signs. They start with glottal stops. Look at our former Prime Minister Blair. He started out by pretending that he could not pronounce his 't's ('a be'er Bri'ain') in a bid to seem young, common and trendy. The nation laughed. By the time we had finished laughing, however, we realised that the disease had taken hold and we were engaged in a full-scale war. Be watchful, and nip it in the bud. So soon as you spot your young using glottal stops, murdering people or eating transfat margarines, take them in hand, or they will be corrupting the young by 'critiquing' texts in front of them and it will all be your fault.

**Crochet** – surprisingly late borrowing (nineteenth century) for knotting (as knitting was known until then) with a hooked needle, from the same diminutive of *croche*, a hook or crook, from which we derive 'crotchet' and 'croquet'.

**Croissant** – a curl of pastry eaten for breakfast. Obviously, the word *croissant* is our 'crescent' and comes from the present participle of the French *croître* and the Latin *crescere*, to grow. So far, so simple. The pastry croissant, however, has spawned a widespread myth. The story goes that a seventeenth-century *pâtissier* was working late into the night in a besieged Vienna when he heard scrabbling sounds, raised the alarm and so confounded a Turkish attempt to mine the walls. The grateful Holy Roman Emperor rewarded the baker with a patent on the pastry of his choice.

He chose the Islamic crescent, wrought in buttery pastry, prospered and became chef to the Emperor's daughter. She in turn married the King of France, bringing her chef and his croissant with her, Paris drooled and the rest is history. This story, however, certainly ain't. Some of those who recount the tale will assure you that the Princess in question was to be Marie Antoinette, which has the pinch of spurious detail characteristic of myth, because, although the dates are a century out, Marie Antoinette was indeed born in Vienna to the Emperor and Empress and did indeed become Queen of France (and, purportedly, left us another legacy in the shape of champagne-glasses, which were modelled on her breasts). Unfortunately, to quote the great Alan Davidson, the croissant 'cannot be traced back beyond the latter half of the nineteenth century at the very earliest', and 'the earliest recipe which corresponds to the modern croissant (dates from) 1905'.

**Croque-monsieur/madame** – *croquer* is a splendid French word for which we have no adequate translation, but 'crunch', 'crack' and 'crisp' are all in there, but with an additional sense of the yielding nature of the thing *croquant*. A *croque-monsieur* (crunch-gentleman) is a toasted (or, to be exact, more commonly roasted) cheese and ham sandwich, a *croque madame* a similar construct, without ham.

**Croquette** – a small roll of chopped meat, fish, potato etc, generally coated in crumbs or some such and fried. Chambers records, 'Curiously, the earliest recorded form of *croquette* in French is 1740, more than three decades after its appearance in English (1706).' Wow. Just think of that. We invented the mini-rissole.

**Crottin** – pungent goat's cheese, made in little discs or balls. A *crottin* is, in fact, a dropping or animal turd.

**Croupier** – one who runs a gaming table, raking in stakes and paying out winnings. Formerly, one who stood behind a gambler, like the loader to a gun, to murmur encouragement, mind his back, supply him with sandwiches etc. Formerly again, one who rode behind a horseman on the horse's 'croup' – whence our 'crupper'.

**Croûte/croûton** – *croûte* is no different from our own 'crust', from the Latin *crusta*, a rind or shell, which is related to the Greek *krystallos*, ice. So a *boeuf en croûte* is a beef in crust, and heaven alone knows why we can't say so. A *croûton*, however, is a small piece of toasted, fried or roasted bread which is used as a vector for other foodstuffs (see *canapé*) or to furnish texture and bear aromatic ingredients in soups and stews and the like. Our own word 'sippet' is far nicer.

**Crudité** – our own word 'crude', from the Latin *crudus*, literally means 'raw', and the word 'raw' itself has figurative connotations of unschooledness and lack of sophistication. Where 'crude' has taken this on as a primary meaning in English, it has retained its original sense in French, so *crudités* are the raw ingredients in salads, dips etc.

**Cuisine** – you just will not believe this. Pumphrey, whom I think I have mentioned as my theoretical collaborator in this work, maintains that *cuisine*, which everyone knows to mean 'kitchen' or 'style of cooking', means, 'So whom have you been going out with?' Bewildering to think that this was once the officer class. *Haute cuisine*, as with *haute couture*, refers to the loftier, finer or more technically ornate branches of cooking, not as Pumphrey insists, the preparation of porridge.

**Cul-de-sac** – well, the word *cul* means, as we are all, regretfully, aware, ‘bottom’, a thing with which the French have always had a most unhealthy preoccupation, and *de sac*, of course, means ‘of a bag’. So a *cul-de-sac* is any street, alley, military position, container etc. with no means of exit save that used for entry.

**Culottes** - divided skirt. Early twentieth century. From French *culottes*, knee-breeches, whence *sans culotte*, a lower-class Parisian republican revolutionary. From the French *cul*, arse, so *culottes* are ‘arselings’, or words to that effect …

***Dada/Dadaist*** – 'Dada' is the French children's word for a hobby-horse. When Jean Arp, the French painter and sculptor, and Tristan Tzara, a Romanian poet, were looking for a name for their new periodical in 1916, they elected this word for its nonsensical sound, and it was adopted to represent a whole radical movement in the arts, now known as Dadaism.

***Danse macabre*** – the dance of death, in which Death plays the pied piper to mankind, leading them to the grave. Macabre, meaning 'grim', 'gruesome' or 'deathly' is a curious word, invariably linked to this dance in its early occurrences. There was an early

French Danse Macabré, which was almost certainly a mediaeval rendition of the dance of the Maccabees, as recorded in II Maccabees 7 in the apocrypha, where the rebellious Jews go to their deaths. In the fifteenth century, we find this represented in English as *The Daunce of Machabree*, which conjures a wondrous picture of Hamish Machabree skirling about the crossed swords. From a misunderstanding of this dance we derive the word 'macabre' and the sense of 'connected to death'.

PAR AVION

**Daube** – stew.

**Débâcle** – unexpected disaster, misfortune or defeat. A late borrowing, first recorded in Thackeray's *Vanity Fair* (1848). Originally from *desbacler*, to set free, from *de* – of or from – and the Latin '*baculum*, a bar or stick, so, to 'unbar' or unshackle. The link between disaster and freedom may seem obscure to all save Iraqis until we look at the modern French meaning of *débâcle*, which is the breaking up of ice in a river and the freeing of the resultant torrent when *solvitur acris hiems*. It is the river, then, which is onomatopoeically freed, and the humans who are subject to resultant disaster.

**Débutant/débutante** – the *but* is usually the end or the target (as in our archers' 'butt'), but it also, curiously, had the sense of a starting point in Old French, perhaps from the more Nordic (or Norman) sense of 'the thick end', as in the butt of a lance or a gun. So a début is here a 'from the beginning', and the noun, as in, 'he made his début in *Uncle Vanya*', has been turned into an infelicitous verb, as in, 'He débuted in...' A débutante is debuting, which is really horrible, and means, in Britain at least, a girl who dresses up like a meringue, curtseys to a cake standing in for the monarch, says 'faaaow' for 'foul' and sleeps with foetal estate agents and crackhead viscounts in order to launch herself on British society.

**Déclassé/e** – 'removed from a class' – so, generally, sunk from a certain social class by dint of *mésalliance* (*qv*), good or ill fortune, large breasts, notoriety etc. Frequently misused to denote 'naff' or 'vulgar' by racially prejudiced and short-sighted pots.

**Décolletage/Décolletée** – I do not see why I should be expected to work with a man who insists that *décolletage* is a rehabilitation process for women addicted to watching reruns of *Gigi*, who are thereafter *décolletées*. A *décolletage* is a low neckline, and one wearing such is said to be *décolletée*. The *collet* here is a diminutive of the French *col*, neck, from Latin *collum*. Necklines rather than hemlines shot up and down in the years between the Norman invasion and the Regency, and *décolletage* has had many a fashionable day since the Middle Ages, including periods, such as during the Elizabethan and Caroline eras, when the throat and the entire breast were exposed, and it is usually thus that the word is today used, implying a neckline so low that it might just reveal a real (or, today, partially real) human mammary.

**Décor** – a genuinely useful, economical word for stage settings or the interior design of showrooms, shops, restaurants and other places of trade, from the Latin *decorare*, to make fitting or suitable, to 'deck out'. Homes should not of course have such things.

**Dégagé** – has two uses in English. Obviously, *dégager* is the opposite of *engager* (from *en gage*, or 'under a pledge'), and both meanings of that word are comprised in its applications here, so, an unattached man or woman may be described as *dégagé(e)'*, as can someone unengaged in work or business, so 'relaxed' or 'laid-back'.

**De haut en bas** – Pumphrey would have me believe that this means 'from a businesslike young woman in stockings', or 'from a woman I met in a drinking establishment', but he is, as usual, wrong, and I cannot think how he arrives at so outlandish an interpretation. This expression evidently means 'patronisingly' or 'from high to low'.

**Déjà entendu/déjà lu/déjà vu** – already understood or heard, already read, already seen. All three terms are frequently used as nouns, as in, 'I read it with a profound sense of *déjà lu*', or, 'I just had an overpowering case of *déjà vu*.' This is often rendered by Pumphrey and, so he says, restaurant critics, as '*déjà* spew', which is just rude. The man's sense of humour is impenetrable.

**Déjeuner** – lunch. Or, rather, breakfast. *Déjeuner* is to break one's fast, but Louis XIV was a slugabed and arose and took his breakfast at noon. Everybody else at Court still had to get up at a respectable hour to urinate, let the dogs out, dust the commodes and so on, so they were compelled to eat a *petit déjeuner* just to keep going until the King decided to have a proper meal. So *dîner*, formerly, as still for children, dogs and northerners, a midday meal, was set back until evening (well, would you like to say, 'Nice lunch, your Majesty?' to a newly awakened Supreme Ruler?), and *déjeuner* for fashionable people became lunch. Now that is power. So we win every war with the French and still they dictate the names of our meals.

**De luxe** – sumptuous, top class, commonly used postpositively when pronounced in the French style – 'an *hôtel de luxe*' – but prepositively in the English form – 'a *de luxe* cabin'. *Luxe* and luxury have always had implicit connotations of disapproval. The Latin *luxuria* means excess no less than sumptuousness, and appears to be derived from luxus, dislocated. By the Middle Ages, *luxurie* was closely associated with lustfulness or wantonness.

**Demi-glace** – nowadays the term is generally used of a basic brown sauce made by slow reduction of beef or veal stock, Madeira, herbs and vegetables. An invaluable article.

**Demi-monde, demi-mondaine** – absolutely NOT 'a small mound or grassy knoll', but the 'half world' or a 'half worldling', a delicate euphemism for the social equivalent of camp-followers – the women (and sometimes, though seldom explicitly stated) men, the 'pretty horsebreakers' and 'dollymops' of Victorian England – who were on the fringes of high society or the *haut monde* or *beau monde*. Some, but not all of these, were prostitutes or courtesans, and, while fêted for their glamour at the theatre or in the park, were seldom welcome at more official public functions. On occasion, our newspapers complain that talentless slatterns are famous for sleeping with footballers or whatever, but it was ever thus, and many a talentless slattern of the *demi-monde*, in my experience, is more amusing, better-groomed and smells better than her *haut monde* sisters. The phrase is sometimes now used of other subcultures whose boundaries overlap those of 'high' society, so 'the sporting demimonde', 'the swinging demimonde' etc.

**Demi-pension** – bed, breakfast and one other meal at a hotel or lodging house. The arrangement made with the proprietor or the cost of that arrangement.

**Demi-vierge** – 'half virgin'. A flighty and flirtatious female who somehow remains a virgin and, when hard-pressed, falls back on her virtue rather than the upholstery. A prick-teaser. These, or their close kin, survive to this day. Though seldom now laying claim to virginity, glamour models and the like revel in a reputation for promiscuity yet invariably blame the males involved for 'undoing' them by wicked wiles.

**Dénouement** – the unravelling of a plot or explanation of its complexities. Not, as commonly supposed, the 'denuding' of a contrived story, but its 'unknotting', from *nouer*, to knot.

**Déraciné(e)** – uprooted or, in Marxian terms, alienated, from *racine*, root, from Late Latin *radicina*, from Latin *radix* (root), ultimately from Indo-European *root wrad* (root) which is also the source of words such as root, wort, licorice, radical, radish, eradicate and ramify. We have the word deracinate, so this is media pundit speak.

**De rigueur** – obligatory, necessary. Literally 'of rigour' or 'of strictness', from Latin *rigor*, stiffness or numbness. I have searched in vain for a contrasting expression which would divide actions into those *de rigueur* and those of something less unbending. It is interesting, however, to observe that the association between stiffness – *rigor* as in *mortis* – and rigour as in strictness or exigence has existed for so long in all three languages.

**Dernier cri** – ah, would that it were! The *dernier cri* or 'last cry' is the latest extravagant demonstration of novelty for novelty's sake. 'Oh, my dear, his frocks are the *dernier cri* in high fashion', or 'this shed with plastic ornamentations is the *dernier cri* in commercial architecture', say the cognoscenti, apparently tragically unaware that someone else is about to screech elsewhere.

**Dernier mot** – 'the last word', only not in our sense as in a mother's 'why must you always have ...?' but much the same as the above, only putatively quieter.

**Derrière** – the bottom, backside, behind or arse. A euphemism of a euphemism. 'Behind' is already an absurd usage, but was not considered suitably prim for some, who resorted to what they had always been taught at school was the French for the preposition 'behind'. As in English, this is not, properly, a noun, and its use tells us far more about the user's psychoses than about the object purportedly described.

**Déshabille, en; Déshabillé(e)** – in a state of undress or undressed, only seldom used with these meanings. Obviously, the term means 'stripped', and originates with *abiller*, which is paradoxically to dress a tree trunk by removing its branches or *billes*. By curious association with *habit*, clothing, however, *habilement* or our 'habiliment' came to mean garment. In general, when we use this term, it is to indicate a state of dishevelment or partial clothing, so Lear on the moor is *en déshabille*, as are the various *soubrettes* (*qv*) and lecherous lovers when surprised in their sweet strivings in innumerable French comedies.

**Dessert** – is absolutely NOT pudding, but that delicious course which follows pudding and, where appropriate, savoury, when the tablecloth is removed and all that has been served is removed or 'de-served', and diners loosen their belts and their tongues, push back their chairs and, around a sunset lake of mahogany, help themselves to fruit, dried fruit, cheese and similar delicacies.

**Détente** – I sometimes wonder from what planet Pumphrey comes. I actually believed that he was contributing something useful when he informed me that he had known a great deal of *entente cordiale* when a Boy Scout at his Hampshire prep-school but also had experience of *détente* when the weather was fine and 'that Mander chap was a bit niffy'. I have since spent several frustrating hours in investigating this claim, but can find no references whatever to scouting. In fact, *détente* is the easing of relations between persons, organisations or nations where once there was contention or tension, as might occur after an apology from the offending party, preferably coupled with prostration and the offer to prepare a decent meal, involving sweetbreads, perhaps, or scallops ...The etymology is self-evident. *Tendere* is Latin for 'to stretch', *detendere* thus to slacken or loosen.

**De trop** – superfluous to requirements. 'You can bring Rose with the turned-up nose but Lulu is *de trop*,' the songwriter might have written, but didn't, for a wide variety of reasons now I come to think about it.

**Diable au corps** – 'the devil in the body'. The persistent or sporadic restlessness or fretfulness which occasions crime, folly, great art, sexual sillinesses and the like. Commonly but mistakenly assumed to be an affliction of the young, but in fact every bit as common and insistent, and far less readily appeased, in older persons.

**Diablerie** – devilment, from the French *diable*, devil, but also and originally dealings with the devil, black magic, sorcery or Satanism. Today just an attractive naughtiness

**Dictionnaire dormant** – 'sleeping dictionary'. The 'sleeping' is here clearly euphemistic or only incidentally apt. The thing itself – a lover who is a native speaker of the language to be learned – is a nigh indispensable aid to language training, and we who have mastered foreign tongues have frequently done so by allowing ourselves, as it coarsely were, first to be mastered by them. It is, perhaps, the very mundanity and predictability of lovers' language, from the '*Mon dieu, oui, donne le moi! Ah, oui, que c'est bon ...!*' to the groans and whimpers in the morning, the occasional curses, the murmured endearments, which makes them immediately comprehensible and memorable and supplies a bedrock for all subsequent learning.

**Dieu et mon droit** – 'God and my right' – as distinct from 'My God, and you're right!' as asserted by Pumphrey and his drinking friends (was this not a Sellar and Yeatman joke?). This is the motto of the British sovereign. A subversive reference to the today generally doubted divine right of kings. Richard I (Coeur de Lion) chose this motto before the victorious Battle of Gisors in 1198. He was identifying the two causes for which he was fighting and the sources of his authority – God, as the supreme authority, and Richard's right to kingship (over France no less than England) because granted by that same God. It was Henry VI who adopted the phrase into the official heraldic arms.

**Dirigisme** – the policy or philosophy of state control or intervention in economic and social matters, the antithesis of liberalism and democracy, and therefore much favoured by left wing administrations. A dirigiste is an advocate of such impertinence, and should be regaled at every opportunity with the following sacred dictum from John Stuart Mill: 'The only purpose for which power can be rightfully exercised over any member of a civilised community, against his will, is to prevent harm to others. His own good, either physical or moral, is not sufficient warrant. He cannot rightfully be compelled to do or forbear because it will be better for him to do so, because it will make him happier, because, in the opinion of others, to do so would be wise, or even right ... The only part of the conduct of anyone, for which he is amenable to society, is that which concerns others. In the part which merely concerns himself, his independence is, of right, absolute. Over himself, over his own body and mind, the individual is sovereign'.

Yee, as our American friends so quaintly but appositely say, ha.

**Discothèque** – a nightclub providing music and lights intended to provoke gut-wriggling, sweating and, at the last, further forms of suppuration *à deux* or, indeed, more. Originally, the word has a far more innocent and placid origin. As a *bibliothèque* or, in the original Italian, *biblioteca*, is a library or book collection, so a *discoteca* is a collection of phonographic records. The early French *discothèques* were cafés or *bistros* where customers could choose which records would be played.

**Distrait/e** – distracted. Perhaps we have retained the French usage for a word which we already possess because of that vague-sounding open diphthong at the end. *Distrahere* is to draw or drag (hence tractors and traction) away or in disparate directions.

**Doctrinaire** – a doctrine is a teaching or body of teaching, a doctor, of course, a teacher. Doctrinaire seems first to have been used of a group which, in 1820, gave its support to constitutional government and a middle-road policy which attempted to reconcile libertarianism and authority – a classic post-Revolutionary fudge. This was universally deemed to be impractical. It was not until the 1870s that this meaning – pedantically theoretical at the expense of practical concerns – entered the English language. Thereafter, the word came to mean, with some justification, authoritarian, unbending, idealistic, opinionated, dumb.

**Dot** – still a matter of some concern to Frenchmen, particularly the nominally noble – a dowry. Both words spring from the same source. We have the Old French *douaire*, which comes from the Latin *dos, dotis*, which is plainly related to *donum*, a gift, and, of course, in the opposite direction again, to our own 'endow'. Traditionally, a *dot* is a marriage portion of which the income is at the husband's disposal while the principal remains part of the wife's family's capital.

**Double entendre** – 'double meaning', a spoken pun or allusion, intentional or unintentional, and usually referring to matters sexual or defecatory. This is a peculiar favourite of the British, although the Americans have lately been catching up as they absorb, as it were, the subtleties of Mrs Slocombe's pussy and the like, in part because English lends itself to such double meanings, in part because broad, even crude popular humour has lived cheek by jowl with high culture in Britain since Chaucer's day as in no other culture. It might be argued that the *double entendre* depends too upon distinction between classes and genders for its success, and that the British have specialised in these. So, for example, Max Miller and George Robey, masters of the genre, were just about acceptable to prurient middle-class men and even to their wives and children, because these last could pretend not to have understood the implications of their words.

**Douce, doucement** – of course, we know *douce* as the feminine form of *doux*, sweet, with its ancient figurative sense of 'pleasant', as in '*dulce et decorum est* …', but occasionally you will hear French fathers purring deep and low to their progeny at the table, '*Doucement, doucement* …', which is to say, 'Gently … calm down … take it easy …' and it is this meaning of *douce* – sober, steady or sage – which persists in Scotland.

**Douche** – a shower or jet of water applied to any part of the body, but most commonly used of such jets when used intrusively to clean southerly cavities. From Italian *doccia*, a shower or conduit, from *docciare*, to pour by drops. This in turn comes from the Latin *doctio*, leading, and *ducere*, to lead, as, of course, does 'conduit', which plainly comes from the French, whereas 'conduct' comes to us direct from the Latin … Oh, dear …

**Doyen/ne** – the leader of a group, the arbiter or model of a discipline or métier. Originally, the leader of ten, from Old French *deien*, derived in turn from the Latin *decanus*, a commander of ten soldiers, monks or whatever, from which we also take our word 'dean'.

**Dressage** – the systematic attempt to turn a free, galloping, leaping, beautiful creature into an automaton, capable of prinking and purposeless contortions. The whole thing is almost as depressing as dog-showing, but the word is quite fun, because, of course, we still 'dress right' on the parade ground, and our word 'dress', now used of apparel, originally had that meaning – to arrange or adjust, as well as to stand up, and was borrowed from the French even then. So 'to dress' became 'to prepare', 'to set in order' (from the Latin *directus*, straight), and subsequently to deck, decorate or dress in clothing. 'Dressage', then, is a throwback to that original sense – training, ordering, preparation.

**Droit de seigneur** – 'the right of the lord', also known as *droit de cuissage* or 'right of thighery' (interfemoral intercourse?), a splendid custom whereby, allegedly, young women of humble birth but less humble manners and appurtenances were afforded the pleasures of their squire's attentions on the night preceding their wedding nights and a lifetime of hasty fumbling from their yokel husbands, so potentially enhancing the gene-pool and teaching the girls a thing or two which they could pass on to their daughters. Alas, the whole thing appears to have been a lubricious invention (though we know of similar provisions in Ghana, for example), but this has never stopped young women from regarding it as their right to couple with young bucks by way of often remunerative practice.

**Duvet** – 'a Jewish party. They have lots of these at *faites vos jeux* in Paris,' asserts Pumphrey. He knows perfectly well, even if he sleeps on a camp-bed, that a duvet is a continental quilt or, as the Americans have it, a 'comforter'. A bag, usually of cotton, filled with down or some artificial substitute, and used as a quick, convenient and effective substitute for blankets and eiderdowns. A reasonably recent innovation in Britain, but far from a new thing. In French, *duvet* means down or fuzz, including the downy hair on forearms and babies' spines.

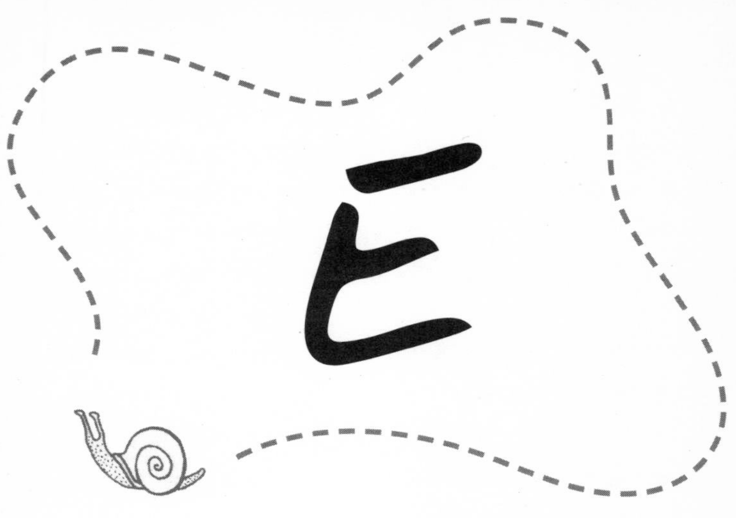


*Eau de Cologne* – a light, rapidly evanescent scent made of alcohol and essential oils, originally made in Cologne. **Eau de Nil** – water of the Nile. A pale green colour romantically considered by the short-sighted and those who have never visited Egypt to resemble the river. **Eau de toilette** – 'toilet water', or, more precisely, water intended for dressing and titivating. A dilute scent. **Eau de vie** – water of life, cognate with the Gaelic *uisge beath* – our 'whisky' – and describing much the same thing. **Eau de vie** is brandy or indeed any liquor distilled from mashes of fruit or aromatics.

**Échangiste** – what is known in English as a 'swinger' and was formerly inaccurately known as a 'wife-swapper' – that is, a person who has sexual relations with a variety of people without gratuitous and immoral emotional commitment in consequence.

**Éclair** – lightning, from Latin *exclarare*, to illumine, light up (the 'ex-' implies darkness), so – and this is a tortuous 'so' – an oblong or tube of choux pastry (*qv*) filled with cream or confectioners' custard, the implication being, at a guess, that the cream bursts from its dark casing like lightning.

**Éclat** – a lovely word, from the French *éclater*, to burst out or to splinter, as of a firework. So, in English, notoriety or scandal and, latterly, fame or brilliant success. Often used loosely as a synonym for *élan* or *panache* (*qqv*) – 'performed with *éclat*' etc.

**Égalité** – only used in English with its brethren in the French revolutionary catchphrase, *Libertée* and *Fraternité*. Since neither *égalité* nor *liberté* has the slightest meaning without substantial qualification, this made a perfect rallying cry with which to lead people to their deaths and those of others.

**Élan** – vivacity, enthusiasm, flair. From *élancer*, to rush or dart, from the Latin *lancea* – a lance or javelin.

**Élite** – a superior or excellent section of a community or society. Precisely synonymous with the term 'elect', in that both words come from the Latin *eligere*, to choose. We actually had the word direct from the Latin as far back as the thirteenth century, but lost it in the fifteenth and reborrowed it from French in the nineteenth. It is now, of course, considered a dirty word by everyone who does not belong to one.

**Embarras de choix/de richesse** – from the same source as 'barrier' and 'barrage', the word 'embarrass' originally meant to hamper or impede. It subsequently came to mean 'to discomfit' or 'to disconcert'. These two phrases retain, perhaps, something of the original meaning, in that an *embarras de choix*, an embarrassment of choices, and an *embarras de richesse*, an embarrassment of wealth or resources, are generally thought of as hindering decision. The phrases are, however, often also used hyperbolically as almost identical terms of approval or delight.

**Embonpoint** – buxomness, plumpness, often once used as a euphemism for 'bust' or 'cleavage'. The word is a phonetic elision of the French phrase *en bon point*, meaning 'in good condition', and is closely related to our own word 'condition'. In the days before we lost touch with animals and with the notion of fitness for a purpose rather than 'fitness' as a non-specific end in itself, measured in large measure by a deficiency of adipose tissue, we would say, 'It's good to see him carrying a bit of condition', or 'If she's planning to get pregnant, she should put on a little condition.' This 'condition' was linked to all the other elements described by this term – brightness of eye, glossiness of coat, bushiness of tail and general wellbeing, but it also meant 'substance', that extra overall weight indicative of good diet and contentment. It did not mean flab or sagging excess flesh. *Embonpoint*, like 'buxomness', has the same unfashionable but delightful implications of approval, admiration and good health.

**Embouchure** – *emboucher* is to place in the mouth. An *embouchure* is the shape of the lips of a wind-instrument player as he or she plays, a factor which in large measure determines that player's distinctive sound. If Satchmo, for example, is inimitable, it is largely because of his entirely peculiar *embouchure*.

**Embrasser** – to embrace or, now, kiss, used in the form, '*Je t'embrasse*' as the closing of a letter, email or telephone call. We who were taught that *baiser* was the French for 'to kiss' are in for a pleasant or unpleasant surprise today, when the word has taken on an altogether more energetic, if not necessarily more intimate, meaning.

**Embusqué** – precisely the same word as our own 'ambushed', from *en* – in and *busche* – bush. The borrowed word, however, slightly amusingly describes one who has dodged military service by obtaining a post in government, the National Guard or some such.

**Émigré** – an emigrant. Of course, this is a pointless borrowing which dates from the days of the French Revolution when the British welcomed so many such from troubled France. No doubt, therefore, this word is quaking as it anticipates my verdict. In this instance, however, I am moved to tolerance. 'Immigrant' and 'emigrant' sound altogether too similar. *Émigré* can relax.

**Éminence grise** – 'grey eminence' – the shadowy figure who wields influence unseen by advising or persuading the more prominently great. Originally, this term was applied to the Grey (because a member of the Capuchin order) monk Père Joseph, the adviser and confidential agent of the far-from-retiring Cardinal Richelieu.

**Emmerdant, emmerder** – intensely annoying or to annoy intensely, from *merde* (*qv*).

**En bloc** – in a group or block. Block is an interesting word, because the French *bloc* meant a chunk of wood, but *blog* is the Irish Gaelic and *ploc* the Scottish for a fragment or chunk, apparently independently. From this earlier meaning comes the sense of 'blocking' as in preventing access by placing blocks in the way, and, in the eighteenth century, the sense of a block of buildings or land. Why we need this foreign version of 'in a block' or 'as a block' is very unclear …

**En brosse** – of hair, cut short and bristly like a brush. Invariably used of menacing characters, usually Teutonic.

**En clair** – 'in clear' or 'in light'. Not in code or otherwise obfuscated.

**Enculer** – to sodomise, bugger, whence the grossly insulting term *enculé*, which simply means 'buggered person', and the graphic *Va te faire enculer chez les Grecs*, which you will often hear called about the Shepherd's Bush area and which means, 'Go and get yourself anally violated among the Greeks', in that the Greeks are still widely associated with this practice by the French.

**En famille** – at home, in the bosom of one's family. Often used to mean 'informally', so: 'No need to dress. We'll just be *en famille*.'

**Enfant terrible** – terrifying, frightful or strange child, holy terror, insufferable brat. I have heard English people struggling with the definition of this term, attempting to wish upon it a euphemistic interpretation, so we are told, '"Terrible" in this context really means "awe-inspiring"'. No, it doesn't. The fact is that we British mistrust and dislike precocity and brats who plague us with questions and taunts, while the French regard such a prodigy as admirable and the above term as approving.

**En fête** – in a state of revelry or celebration. *See* Fête.

**En masse** – absolutely not 'during religious service', any more than *en titre* is 'mid-snigger' as was scrawled here. Please ignore all this puerile drivel. *En masse* means, of course, in a mass, in a body, as a whole …

**Ennui** – some would translate this as 'boredom', but *ennui*, as well as being 'annoyance' or irritation' has overtones of *accidie*. It is a spiritual state of being rather than the sort of thing of which ill-bred and -fed children complain when their televisions cease to function (why has no-one invented a television powered by pedal-operated dynamo?) Interestingly, the word is precisely the same as our own 'annoy', which springs from the French *anoier* or *enoier*, which comes in turn from the Latin *in odio* – 'in hatred'. **Ennuyant** is just boring or aggravating.

**En passant** – in passing, 'by the by '…

**En plein air** – in the open air. Revolutionary method of painting, invented, with their usual startling originality, by the Impressionists, who sneered at academic contemporaries who actually worked in their studios. Turner, of course, had done the same thing years before, but in English, so it did not count. You will sometimes hear this expression needlessly used of other activities such as eating and fornication, in which case *alfresco* – in the fresh (air) – is prettier and more succinct.

**En premières noces** – in a first bid at marriage. A conventional term in French biographical summaries, presumably adopted into English because the words 'first' and 'marriage' were considered disreputable in conjunction.

**En primeur** – fresh, new (of wine), young, before bottling.

**En principe** – in principle. Pointless and irritating affectation.

**En route** – on or along the way. So, 'I am *en route* to Macclesfield and there is a delightful restaurant *en route* ...' Route is quite an interesting and ancient word, actually, and tells us something of how roads were once built, because it comes from *rupta*, past participle of *rumpere*, to break, as in 'rupture' and the like, because, of course, that is what our roads once were – strips of land broken up into small fragments readily compressed by traffic.

**Ensemble** – a group of people or objects working in unison or harmony to an end. This sense is enshrined in the word's origin – *in simul* – simultaneously, 'all together now'. Often used adjectivally of a piece of music, film or other work, meaning 'not a tedious star vehicle created by a committee, but a work performed by a group to the greater enjoyment of the viewer or listener and the greater integrity of the creator's vision', a disgracefully outdated notion, at least in Britain and the United States. As a noun, 'ensemble' is also often used of combinations of apparel.

**En suite** – well, *suite* comes from *suivir*, to follow, which, like 'suit', in turn comes from the Latin *sequor* and its past participle *secutus* (*sequitus*), to follow or attend upon. In gracious and graceful days in which we were concerned with vistas and sequences of aesthetic experiences in gardens and houses, 'suite' was adopted to signify a series of connected rooms following one upon the other, so 'in sequence' as the best translation. 'Suit' was already English for matching clothes in the livery of attendants – hence also 'suits' of playing cards. From the connecting rooms came the furniture which was also designed to be seen in sequence and the musical compositions intended similarly to be enjoyed.

Returning, however, somewhat breathlessly, to the rooms, the word came to be used – inappositely, for our more stationary 'set' is far more appropriate – of connecting rooms in hotels and lodgings. Bathrooms were generally located along the corridor from the bedroom, and guests had to grope their way thither and queue or, more agreeably, get lost and find themselves inadvertently blundering into others' bedrooms. Slowly but surely, however, since the Edwardian period (I remember my grandmother commenting on the innovation at the blessed Goring), hoteliers have afforded guests bedrooms with their own private bathrooms which they have described as *en suite*, and builders of homes in places like Esher and Weybridge have followed – as it tautologically were – suit, so that estate agents now routinely describe attached bathrooms as *en suites*.

**Entente, entente cordiale** – an *entente* is an understanding or agreement (from *entendre*, intend, so 'what is intended') usually between states. An *entente cordiale* is a warm and heartfelt one, just as a drink called a 'cordial' is 'for the heart', from the Latin *cor*, *cordis*, heart.

**Entourage** – from *entourer*, to surround, so a group of hangers-on, courtiers, gofers, flatterers, makeweights and other necessary accessories for celebrity without cerebration.

**Entr'acte** – an interval between acts in a drama. Now used, if at all, of cigarettes, snacks or even conversations enjoyed between bouts of sexual activity.

**Entrechat** – I don't care what the boy says ('I think you'll be surprised by what he can contribute'. Well, he was certainly right there!) I am not going to reproduce Pumphrey's interpretation of this word. What he describes is disgusting, illegal, inhumane and probably impossible, and I have no reason to believe, as he maintains, that it is widespread in the Pyrenees. When I explained that an *entrechat* was a classical ballet term, he replied,'Well, there you are. Chappies who can prink around with *poussins* shoved down their pants would do anything'. Smothering my revulsion and outrage at this calumny, I explained very patiently that the word denotes an upward spring or leap in which a dancer twiddles his feet or strikes them together with his arms aloft. Pumphrey's reply? 'Not surprised. Those cats know how to look after themselves ...

**Entrecôte** – literally 'between ribs'. A sirloin steak, cut from behind the shoulder of a beef animal.

**Entrée** – outdated term still to be found on the menus of particularly bad Railway Hotels, apparently denoting 'main courses' or 'meat courses'. Nothing illustrates better the absurdity of French terminology ignorantly used, supposedly to afford some spurious *cachet*. The *entrée* (literally the 'beginning' or 'entry') used to be the third course, following the fish or soup and the *relevé* or intermediate course. It was usually some sort of sauced dish (or several dishes) or casserole of meat or fish, and, in turn, preceded the *rôts* or roasts, usually of poultry or game, the salad, the final savoury course, the puddings and the dessert (*qv*). The term is today wholly useless in French and positively laughable in English.

**Entrepreneur** – please use this word correctly. I have seen criminals and the parents of multiple-birth children describing themselves as 'unemployed entrepreneurs' or 'unemployed property developers', which surely describes all of us when out of a job. An *entrepreneur* is one who undertakes (*entreprendre*) risk and sole responsibility for a project. He or she is not a jumped-up manager or lucky employee in a public company, but a creative person who controls an entire business from its germination to its fruition or demise.

**Épater les bourgeois** – also known as shooting a fish in a barrel in that the bourgeois are, by definition, so easily *épatés* or shocked. The Regency knew this as 'bamming' – the deliberate attempt to invoke disapproval for comic or even, occasionally, artistic effect. *Épatant les bourgeois* became a defining sport of the artistic community at the end of nineteenth century, when artists emulated the moral relativism and frankness of their aristocratic predecessors and the bourgeois were at their most insecurely absolutist and unimaginative. Today, formerly natural pastimes such as eating meat, hunting, expressing desire, disapproval or distaste and occasional heterosexual activity are sufficient to cause the bourgeois to suffer paroxysms. It is still fun.

**Escargot** – edible snail. From a Provençal word, *escaragol*, derived in turn, it seems, somewhat improbably, from the Latin *scarabaeus*, beetle, which in turn comes from the Greek *karabos* which served both for beetle and for crayfish.

**Espièglerie** – prankishness, mischievousness, playfulness. A weird and picturesque etymology, this one. The word – a favourite of Wodehouse – is said to be derived from the Dutch *ull*, owl, and *spiegel*, mirror (from Latin *speculum*, of course). Hence the mischievous German folk-hero Till Eulenspiegel or Owl Mirror. Well, I don't know …

**Ésprit de corps** – team or group spirit, readiness to subsume individual interests to the welfare of the family, regiment or other group.

**Ésprit de l'escalier** – literally 'the wit of the staircase', an indispensable phrase for the witticisms and retorts which elude one at the dinner table or over drinks but spring to mind only when they have lost the immediacy essential to wit.

**Étiquette** – correct or conventional behaviour, accepted manners or protocol of a society, profession or other social group. A most interesting word, in that our 'that's the ticket' comes from 'that's the etiquette', which one might think a pun, but the original meaning of etiquette actually was 'a ticket or label'. It is uncertain just how the word came to acquire its new meaning in the eighteenth century, but it is suggested that invitations or 'tickets' to the Court came, as do invitations to royal garden parties to this day, with instructions as to decorum and approved conduct. The words *etiquet* and 'ticket' come from *estiquer* and 'stick', in that a ticket or label was affixed to a door, package or decapitated envoy for dispatch or display.

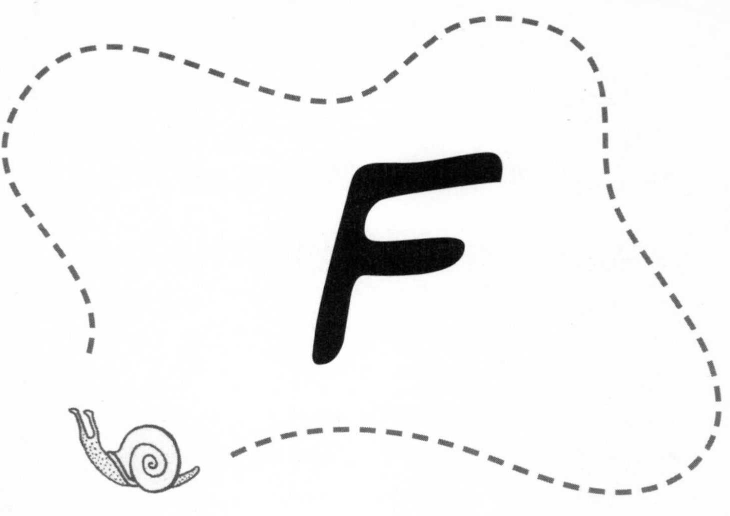


**Fait accompli** – accomplished fact or deed, generally used of something effectively irrevocable or, at least, that the speaker wishes to maintain to be so.

**Farce** – stuffing or forcemeat, hence *farci* of the food so stuffed, from Latin *farcire*, which has the same meaning. Whether our 'forcemeat' is an English adaptation of 'farce-meat' or was always 'meat to be forced', I cannot say, though the former seems very much more likely. From this we get the sense of 'farce' as a comic play involving a deal of action and loose underwear and women, because such plays, essentially closer to dumbshow than drama, were the light relief to Mystery plays, 'stuffed' into the improving dramas as interludes in order to draw audiences and leaven moralism.

**Farouche** – one of the few borrowings which is truly indispensable, *farouche* denotes a state of mind and body rendered paradoxical by the failure of English to integrate its meanings in a word. It means savage yet timorous, wild yet captive, fierce and sullen yet inspiring protectiveness. Imagine a weasel in a trap, scared and trembling yet at any moment ready to try to rip your throat out, or your teenage daughter when she comes home off her face and needing a cuddle. It is a very necessary word, which comes to us from *forus* – outdoors – as in Archbishop Stigant's famous pun about the *forestarii* or foresters: 'Who are they?' he demanded about some people waiting in an anteroom. '*Forestarii,*' he was told. '*Foris stent*', (they stand outside), said Stigant. I still chuckle at that one late in the night, as, I am sure, do you.

**Faute de mieux** – for want of a better alternative. *Faute* is a want or deficiency, from *fallita*, past participle of *fallere*, to disappoint, fail or deceive. In English, the word regained its 'l' in the Middle Ages, giving us the sense of shortcoming or fault and, of course, (*fallere* also went *falsus*) 'false', meaning deceitful or fake. Pumphrey says that *faute de mieux* means 'it was the cats who knocked it over'. He has now gone to sleep in his armchair and is making a noise like a double bass dragged over gravel.

**Fauve/Fauvism** – everyone knows that Matisse, Derain and their ilk were called Fauvistes because a critic declared in 1915 of a classical sculpture amidst their paintings, '*Donatello au milieu des fauves!*' – 'Donatello surrounded by wild beasts', and that *fauve* means wild beast. And so it does, but the word has a more interesting and, as it turns out, wholly inapposite origin. Matisse and Co. were, of course, known for the brilliance of their colours, but *fauve* is French for a dull hue akin to our 'fawn', 'dun' or 'fallow'. Now, this word came to be used for a whole class of animals with such coats, including lions, cheetahs, tigers and so on, so that the section of the zoo dedicated to them came to be known as the *fauverie*'. The misguided critic was therefore actually describing brilliant canvases as 'dun-coloured animals', which is neither witty nor accurate.

Moving on from this, just for interest's sake, there was a fourteenth-century satirical ballad *Le Roman de Fauvel*, in which Fauvel (the equivalent of our calling an animal 'Brownie' or some such) was a treacherous, cunning, leery pig of a dun horse. This poem enjoyed great popularity in Renaissance Britain, in which *fauve* meant next to nothing, and the notion of soothing or cajoling the vicious beast to be obliging came to be expressed by the phrase 'to curry' – that is, to brush or comb (we still have curry-combs in every tack-room) 'Fauvel', whence our otherwise curious expression 'to curry favour'.

PAR AVION

**Faux/faux naïf/faux pas** – *faux* is false or fake, from *fallere* as in *faute de mieux* above. So we have revolting things called '*faux* fur' and '*faux* leather', for example, favoured by those people who would really rather that we had no cause to have any animals at all, or, in the case of '*faux* leopard', for example, by those who actually wish to preserve specific animals but also quite like their style. Occasionally, you come across '*faux* leatherette', which causes the mind to reel. Presumably the French word is used because, to those who do not speak French, it sounds 'nicer' than 'fake' or 'false'. *Naïveté* (*qv*) is not generally thought of as a desirable quality save, for some reason, in children, young women deficient in melanin and peasants, in whom it is thought charming to believe in fairies, true love and the like, to paint as though with the feet and to sing like a Spice Girl or an unoiled gate. For all that, there is a class of indulgent art collectors, ignorant animal buyers, grandparents and others who esteem the *naïf* above sophistication. The *faux naïf* are there to satisfy them, assuring them that they love them with all their hearts and parts, that their hair is spun of fairy gold, that their spavined nags regularly win the Derby and that their carefully wrought matchstick men and pigs shaped like balloons are in fact genuine folk art. As a general rule, except with the mentally deficient, all *naïveté* is *faux*, and the innocent little child is looking to feed his face, and the chromatically challenged young lady and the peasant to fill his or her bank account or to gratify the exigent groin.

Finally, to *faux pas*, which simply means 'false step' – a solecism or act which offends against convention, as notably celebrated by the great H.R. Bateman. Pumphrey has woken up and insists that he had lots of *faux pas* and had to call them 'uncle' when he bumped into them in the corridor at night. He really can be quite sweet sometimes ... A dangerously little knowledge of French has changed the sense and common usage of this expression, with people stating that this or that is 'an absolute *faux pas*', by which they mean 'no-no' or prohibition. This is evidently derived from *Il ne faut pas* – it must not be – a total veto. Ninety per cent of my acquaintance – generally educated people – believe this to be the origin of the phrase.

**Femme fatale** – a fatal woman, or woman whose charms are such that poor, susceptible men must fear for their lives or their virtue – which, of course, they hold dearer – the poor, susceptible little dears. The notion that it is the woman who, by reason of her beauty and allure is fatal is similar to that which holds whisky responsible for drunkenness.

**Fête/fête champêtre** – a fête in England is, for once to quote Pumphrey with approval, 'a bizarre event considerably worse than death', generally dedicated to raising funds and the esteem of dry old ladies in holy hats. In France, however, it is a joyous party or festival or mixture of the two, generally prolonged and involving music, games, often costume, fireworks, feasting and other jollities. The *fête champêtre* is in fact the commonest variety, as idyllically recorded in Alain Fournier's *Le Grand Meaulnes* – a fête held outdoors in a rural environment. 'To fête' someone, of course, is to celebrate or honour him, though the phrase is most commonly used passively – 'justly fêted for his brushwork' or some such.

**Fiancé/e** – one engaged to be married, originally from Latin *fidus*, faithful and Middle Latin *affidare*, to trust.

**Filet** – yes, *horribile dictu*, there are people – usually property developers and owners of Rolex watches – who use this word for a fillet of beef – 'I will have (or, still worse, "take") the filet.' Such people should have their heads held in ice-buckets until all their strivings cease and their long struggles with insanity are mercifully over. The word 'fillet', meaning 'thin strip or slice' and derived from a diminutive of *fil*, thread, has existed very comfortably in English for many centuries. From this we derive the sense of 'to fillet' – that is, to remove from the bone and gristle, and so 'fillet of fish' or 'fillet steak'. Besides which, Pumphrey informs me that his joke about the fisherman's daughter and the wet plaice does not work if the absurd French pronunciation be used.

**Film noir** – 'black film', a style of film popular in the late 1940s, characterised by atmospheric, sombre lighting, urban settings, delicious wicked villainnesses, solitary, sardonic heroes and the best scripts ever written. *Double Indemnity* is, perhaps, the noble touchstone of the genre, which is still imitated, sadly in unrealistic colour and shot on location rather than in the studio, to this day.

**Fin de siècle** – 'end of century'. Despite the best efforts of journalists, we really did not have a *fin de siècle* at the end of twentieth century, which simply fizzled out like a squib on a damp dungheap. The meaning therefore remains that of the end of the nineteenth century and the style of the time, which was characterised by self-conscious but dubious 'decadence', ornate and laborious 'style', a great deal of Swedenborg which it could have done without, sexual ambivalence, *épatant* of *les bourgeois* (*qv*), silly costume and talk about art rather than its creation. All great fun.

**Finesse** – subtlety, delicacy, style, a delicate strategy. 'To finesse' is to try to take a trick in whist or bridge with a card lower than another held, although the card played is not in sequence with the card in the hand. I really do not know what I am talking about, but have just had to trust Pumphrey here, God help me.

**Flâneur/flânerie** – a *flâneur* is one who saunters along urban streets, observing and being observed. *Flânerie* is his (usually his for obvious reasons) avocation and the philosophy which motivates him in his wanderings. Baudelaire was the high priest of *flâneurs*, yet, unlike many another of this calling who prides himself upon his idleness, he turned his observations to brilliant creative use. Beerbohm Tree speaks of young men of the period going for 'a slope down Bond Street', plainly a normal activity for Mayfair *flâneurs*, but sloping has not proved to have the longevity of *flânant*.

**Folie à deux, folie de grandeur, folie du doute** – *folie* wants the jolliness of our 'folly', which merely means silliness or foolish behaviour or, of course, a wholly purposeless, generally diverting and sometimes enchanting building. The French version means psychosis or obsession, which is not really as appropriate, in that the root source, the Latin *follis*, means bellows, hence windbag, hence idiot or, of course, professional fool, which is all really a joke.

**Folie à deux** is a terrifying madness of which we all have some experience, God help us, but which, in its most pathological form, has wrought terrible evil. The extreme case in recent times is probably that of the Moors murderers, Myra Hindley and Ian Brady, who might have been almost reasonable people had they not met one another and shared gross appetites and delusions. **Folie de grandeur** or 'madness of greatness' is commoner, and is to be found among mummers who believe themselves to be their roles, footballers and other monied persons without wit who believe themselves to be important, persons in uniform or official positions who believe their uniforms and positions afford them intellects and authority which they do not possess, cartoon characters who believe themselves to be Napoleon and all people who 'work' for telecommunications companies. The fool was the traditional nostrum against such folly in kings and emperors, but the fool is now king, and the sons and daughters of kings are content to play gentle fools. **Folie du doute** is also common but more comprehensible and, generally, justifiable, and would be welcome in all of the above. It is the paralysis caused by persistent self-doubt.

**Fonctionnaire** – a functionary or civil servant, generally afflicted with *folie de grandeur* as above.

**Fondant** – literally 'melting', from *fondre* and, previously, Latin *fundere*, to melt or pour, whence, of course, our own 'foundry'. A fondant is a sweet or confection made with sugar, egg white and enormous effort. A fondant potato, however, is cooked slowly in butter until tanned and wrinkled on the outside and soft and powdery within.

**Fondue** – or 'melted', is one of the most indigrestible foodstuffs known to humankind, being composed of melted cheese (usually Raclette), wine and, often, kirsch, into which chunks of bread are dunked. Generally associated with Switzerland, this has given rise to an enormously intricate barrage of equipment – pans or crocks, spirit heaters, twin-tined forks and 'Lazy Susans', or carousels divided into neat little compartments – which ranks with the 'sandwich-toaster' among the most-given and least-used wedding presents. Fondue is deceptively palatable after a day of slithering on the slopes, and is said to contribute to a sense of communal goodwill similar, no doubt, to that experienced by hyaenas or women who have chewed on the same bone. The same name is given by association to *fondue bourguignonne*, which I do not believe to be Bourguignonne at all, and which is a poor man's *Bagna Caoda*, in which cubes of steak, again on forks, are dipped by diners in a central pot or pan of hot oil. *Fondue* is also for some reason an alternative name for *chiffonade* (*qv*) of various vegetables for inclusion in sauces and soups, but this is simply perverse.

**Force majeure** – a greater force.

**Fou rire** – 'mad laughter'. The fit of irresistible hilarity which generally visits us at funerals and other solemn occasions.

**Foyer** – hearth, probably best understood today as the kitchen and so the centre, or focus of activity, and the word is in fact derived from the Latin '*focus*', meaning 'hearth'. From this has come the sense of a large room in which patrons of a theatre foregather and mingle (some old theatres still have fireplaces in their foyers) and so, by inappropriate association, the word has come to denote the entrance hall of a public building.

**Fracas** – a disturbance, *contretemps* or noisy squabble or skirmish. *Fracassare*, to smash to smithereens, the Italian origin, is surely onomatopoeic, and it is speculated that it is formed of *frangere*, to break and *quassare* to shatter. By the time that the word reaches French, however, it has lost all such immediacy. The word retains usefulness only in that it denotes the noisiness rather than the gravity of the confrontation.

**Frisée** – totally pointless borrowing, usually applied to varieties of chicory or other salads and meaning 'frizzy' or 'curly'. Since we have 'frizzy' and 'frizzle' (to curl), both from the same source (*friser* is to curl, and is thought, rather charmingly, to come from *frire*, to fry), this is a pretentious absurdity.

**Frisson** – this, on the other hand, is a necessary and good word, best translated by our own 'thrill', but with 'shiver' or 'shudder' built in. A *frisson* is habitually, though not necessarily, pleasurable, and may result from the first whisky of the evening, a tongue-tip or a dread swarming up the spine, martial music, warmth of a winter's evening, an unexpected smile from across a crowded art gallery, a snatch of 'La Vie en Rose' heard from a passing convertible … Yes, well. It is a bitter-sweet shudder …

**Frottage** – from *frotter*, to rub. A decidedly sad and deviant practice of rubbing your person against another's in pursuance of sexual gratification, usually in a crowded tube train or some such. Known in certain circles as 'a dry hump'.

**Frou-frou** – well, what other noise do skirts (full skirts, not slivers of fabric) make beneath the strains of music in a ballroom, or straw when tossed in a stable? 'Possibly imitative of the sound', says Chambers, as the pontiff is possibly Papist …

**Fuselage** – the body or torso of an aeroplane. From the same source as 'fuse' for a bomb or electrical circuit, to whit, *fusus*, a spindle, owing to the tube shape common to all.

***Gaffe*** – a social blunder or solecism. Now why is a gaffe such an error in French and English alike when the source word in both means 'boat-hook', whence our own 'gaff' for landing fish? I confess that I have no idea, and nor has Pumphrey, who is thinking of going off to Scotland for a few days and seems concerned that I will be unable to do this work without his learned input. Frankly, the notion of continuing in an empty house without the distraction of his fatuous suggestions and often crude jokes is delightful.

***Gamin, gamine*** – a street urchin, whence all the pert, tart, chirpy, scruffy, wily qualities associated with

such a creature. While the thing itself may be unattractive, haircuts, fashions, personalities and manners described as *gamin* are often enchanting. The origins of the word are obscure.

**Gâteau** – a rich, layered cake such as the infamous 'Black Forest' variety, frequently served as a pudding in the 1950s and 1960s and so known in order to avoid the sturdy yeoman word 'cake', which sounds altogether too commonplace for such a function. Poor 'cake', a Nordic word of great antiquity which has served over millennia to denote alike confections of enormous beauty and ornateness and everyday, homely items, and yet in the twentieth century was considered, perhaps because of its simple sound, perhaps because of its associations with soap and the like, altogether too plain to serve for the latest stratified extravagance of cream, buttercream, confectioners' custard, liqueurs, fruit, sweeties and flavourings whose strata are none other than simple – cake. The word *gâteau* (which comes from the Old French *guastrel* meaning fine flour), should be eschewed at every turn, and those who use it spurned and refused sexual favours until they are better.

**Gauche, gaucherie** – *gauche* is 'left' and *droite*, 'right', so 'gauche' is awkward or inept while 'adroit' and 'dexterous', for example, mean skilled and adept. At this, as at the connotations of the Latin for left, *sinister*, left-handed people become very excited and protest at prejudice, pointing with pride to famous left-handers such as Jack the Ripper (who was certainly sinister – and adroit – but was not in fact left-handed), the Boston Strangler, Napoleon, Gerald Ford, Ronald Reagan, Bart Simpson and people like that, all of whom have excelled in their peculiar fields. They are, of course, absolutely er … right.

The thing is that *droite*, like *droit*, comes from the Latin *directus*, straight, and that the two words have remained linked throughout the centuries just as we have retained the common meanings of the word 'right' – straight, true or correct, just claim or entitlement and the right-hand side, and the sense of 'left' implicit in its origin, the Old English *lyft*, as 'weak' or 'clumsy'. This is not motivated by scorn for the left-handed but by the majority's perception of themselves. For most of us, our right hands and feet are strong and capable and our left weak and clumsy. *Gaucherie* is generally just social ineptitude or *naïveté*.

**Gêné, gênée** – embarrassed.

**Genre** – a variety, type or class, usually of painting, books. The same word as our own 'gender' (the two were linked in Middle English as *gendre*) and springs from the same source (*genus, generis*) as countless other words and borrowings such as generation, general, generic, generous, gens and genus.

**Gigot** – leg, of lamb etc. or sleeve of the same shape. A little 'hopper', from *giguer*, to hop, skip or frolic, whence also *gigolette*, dancing girl, and *gigolo*, dancing partner, and, of course, 'jig'.

**Gilet** – a waistcoat, apparently from the Turkish.

**Gîte** – a lodging or stopping-off point on a journey, or, more commonly today, a furnished holiday home, from Old French *gist*, a lodging or home.

**Glace, glacé, glacée** – glace means 'ice', and is absurdly used by some people to mean ice-cream. *Glacé/e* therefore means crystallised, as in *marrons* or chestnuts, or slick, shiny, glossy or 'glazed' as in leather or silk, though the links between glossy, gleam, glass, glaze, glow and the like are infinitely complex and ancient.

**Gourmand** – glutton or gluttonous. Of uncertain origin. Pumphrey left on the 11.29 train. The house seemed to sigh. And now we are racing ahead with this important work.

**Gourmet** – I am delighted to be able to tell you, for example, that extensive research has yielded none but imitative or accidental links between this word, which means 'connoisseur of food' or 'gastronome' and *gourmand* above, because *gourmet* comes from *gromme*, the Old French word for a wine-taster, and retained this meaning until the nineteenth century when, probably by association with *gourmand*, a word in common use for far longer, it was adapted to bear its modern sense. The association is false, because a *gourmet* is never a *gourmand* and *vice versa*.

**Grande passion** – great, overwhelming, incomparable passion. Curiously, you never hear this phrase used of a current relationship, but only of one in the distant past, with which, it is invariably implied, the present cannot compare – 'He was my *grande passion*', they say, or, 'That was the year of my *grande* *passion.*' Pumphrey – and this was another cause of our rift – coarsely said, 'Of course, what she is really saying is, that at that time she felt really good. Her breast filled her brassière (*qv*) and her allowance her bank account to a nicety, her gusset was agreeably damp, she was admired by many who did not know her and adored by at least one who had money and just enough time but not too much to devote to her. There were no children, creditors or publishers nagging her and she had no possessions save some pretty frocks and trinkets. She could devote herself entirely to loving and being loved. In short, the so-called "*grande passion*" is a concept bred of nostalgia for a thousand prelapsarian things, not one person at all. Grand passion, my arse!' Small wonder, I think you will agree, that I am glad to be rid of so insensitive and uncomprehending a person.

**Grand-Guignol** – a book, film or play featuring a series of ghoulish or blackly comic events, from a puppet show of this kind – not unlike our Punch and Judy but wanting the domestic realism – which was popular with French children and originated at the Grand Guignol theatre.

**Grand Prix** – Pumphrey has here written, incomprehensibly, *'Grand Prix (ejac and then some). I say, what splendid chaps!'* I see no connection whatever between this nonsensical supposed definition and the real one, which is, of course, that *Grand Prix* simply means 'big prize', and is now used for the race or contest in which such a prize may be won.

**Grand seigneur** – great or grand gentleman, and the manners, customs and attitudes associated with the same. *Seigneur*, which means lord or lord of the manor, comes from *senior*, the comparative of the Latin *senex* – old.

**Gratin** – commonly believed to mean a dish in which everything is soused in cheese sauce, but in fact any dish topped with scrapings or gratings of anything to provide a crust.

**Grimoire** – a primer or manual of dark arts, thought to be derived from the word 'grammar' deliberately or accidentally misspelled.

**Gueule de bois** – 'mouth of wood'. Hangover.

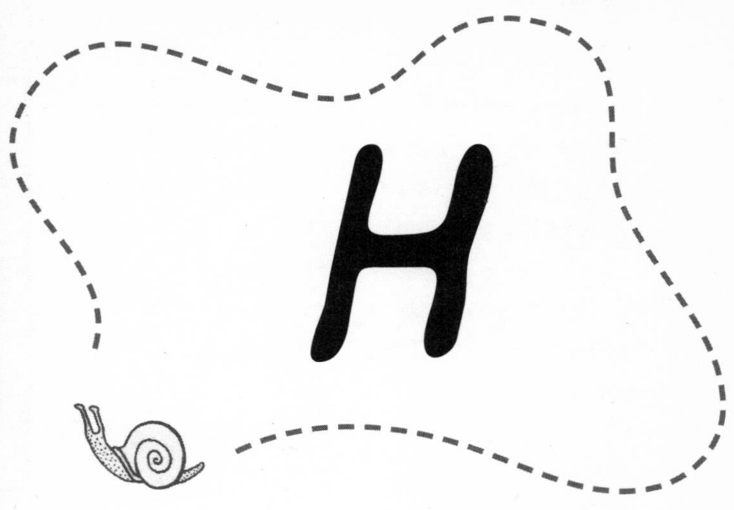


***Habitué*** – a regular visitor or resident, from *habituer*, to accustom or habituate. Um, that's it.

***Haute couture*** – see **Couture**.

***Haute cuisine*** – see **Cuisine**.

***Haut monde*** – 'high world' – the fashionable world, as opposed to the *demi-monde* (*qv*).

***Hauteur*** – loftiness, whence haughtiness, the English version of the word with precisely the same meaning and origin.

**Homme sérieux** – 'serious man', or, rather, a man to be taken seriously, a man of his word, the sort of person that you can do business with, not a frivolous waste of space.

**Honi soit qui mal y pense** – 'evil be to him who thinks ill'. It is quite evident that Pumphrey was inebriated when writing his contributions to this section of the book. I have considered his interpretation of this, the motto of the Order of the Garter, from every point of view, and can make no sense of it whatever. It reads, 'Honey has taken up the management of a Pakistani male prostitute'.

**Hors concours** – I am not even going to tell you what was written here. The notion of such women even having races in those heels and tight skirts is silly. The phrase means 'in a class of its own', 'in a different league', 'beyond competition', so so far superior that, while others may compete, that which is *hors concours* or, literally, 'out of contention', has already won the laurels.

**Hors de combat** – again, I cannot be bothered with my collaborator's input and need not, now that he is plaguing the Scots, even argue with him. Although females were generally *hors de combat* or 'out of the battle' by reason of their gender, camp-followers were a great deal closer to the front line than most women. *Hors de combat* means injured, indisposed, disqualified or otherwise debarred from involvement, not merely in a fray but in any activity.

**Hors d'oeuvre** – 'outside the work'. It is this which once made sense of *entrée* (above), in that an *hors d'oeuvre* was considered a superfluous addition or prelude to the carefully planned *oeuvre*, the schematised, themed work of art which is a meal, while the *entrée* was then the first course. An *hors d'oeuvre* was thus similar to today's *amuse-gueule* (*qv*).

**Hotel particulier** – not an hotel but a private town house or palace, called *particulier* because it is (or rather was), so far from being an hotel, exclusive and in private ownership.

**Idée fixe** – an obsessive or immoveable idea, a monomania.

**Idée reçue** – a *Guardian* reader's opinion.

**Idiot savant** – a 'knowing' or 'wise idiot'. As portrayed by Dustin Hoffman in *Rain Man*, an *idiot savant* can memorise whole telephone directories, rail timetables, volumes of Shakespeare and the like without the least understanding as to how to use the data. Nevertheless, a signal illustration of what we can achieve if we can focus the mind and banish vague yearnings and distracting imaginings. I, for example, might have memorised and completed this book in a mere month, had it not been that the mind and body decline to function as a coherent, dedicated unit. The word 'idiot', by the way, originally meant a layman or unskilled person, as distinct from what today we would call a 'specialist'. It need hardly be pointed out that we are far more likely to find instructive wisdom in an ignorant person than in a specialist, and that many modern specialists are as inapplicably knowledgeable as the Asperger's (the condition most commonly associated with this term) sufferers. Oh, dear, I am plainly distracted today.

**Impair** – as opposed to *pair*. Odd, of numbers. Not one of a pair.

**Impromptu** – extempore or improvised, though the original sense of the Latin phrase *in promptu* was 'in readiness', which describes most impromptu, off-the-cuff witticisms far more accurately.

**Ingénu/e** – an innocent, *naïf* person, usually female and so in the form *ingénue*, a dramatic role of such a character, or, by association, an actor or actress commonly associated with such roles. Our 'ingenuous' is the same word, but has retained the sense of frankness without that of vulnerability implicit in the French borrowing.

**Insouciant/insouciance** – to be *insouciant* is to be carefree, though not necessarily careless. The Old French *soucier* means 'to trouble' and comes from the Latin *sollicitare*, to disturb or agitate. *Insouciance* is thus a desirable if deluded state of mind.

**Instant/moment critique** – the critical or decisive moment, the turning-point. 'Critique' and 'critical' come to us from the same source as 'crisis', although their meanings have become so distinct that a headline such as 'Man Crushed by Train Critical' is usually greeted with giggles and comments such as, "Well, he would be, wouldn't he?". So this is the moment of crisis or irrevocable transition, the point of no return.

***J'accuse*** – Pumphrey actually claimed when we were going through these words that he was at school with J'accuse and his younger brother Will. What am I to do with the man? He is quite absurd. *J'accuse*, of course, were the opening words of Emile Zola's letter to *L'Aurore*, lambasting the military authorities for the disgraceful persecution of Jewish officer Alfred Dreyfus, his wrongful conviction for treason and the subsequent whitewash. Zola's letter reopened the case and proved Dreyfus's innocence. The words have come to be used of similarly dramatic articles or speeches of accusation, so, 'He finally delivered his devastating *J'accuse* after he had eliminated the possibility that Miss Scarlet had done it with the lead piping in the library.'

**Jadé/e** – jaded. Mildly amusing camp coining from a non-existent French word. 'I am feeling a little *jadé* today' is really quite poignant and amusing.

**J'adoube** – 'I repair'. Standard chess term meaning, 'I intend to touch this piece without its being counted a move.' My libidinous Russian acquaintance Dmitri used to say this to female strangers in Totnes. He was really quite shocked when the British courts refused to accept it as a defence.

**Jalousie** – an early form of Venetian blind, common in tropical climes, made up of horizontal slats which can be raised or lowered to permit or obstruct the passage of light or air. From an earlier French word denoting a lattice screen through which one may see but not be seen, hence, given the French preoccupation with infidelity and *amour propre* (*qv*), its name, 'jealousy'.

**Jardinière** – 'female gardener'. A large pot, generally elevated, intended to hold growing plants. *Jardinières* tend to be *cache-pots* (*qv*).

**Jejune** – doesn't even belong here in that it is not a French word at all – or rather, there is an Old French word, *jejune*, but it is unrelated to our own jejune, which comes direct from the Latin and means dull, boring, featureless, where the Latin *jejunus* means atrophied or hungry. There is a strange usage, however of a word frequently misspelt 'jejeune', which is assumed, as with *bibelot* (*qv*) to be a burbling, childlike compounding of *jeune*, young, and to mean derisibly *naïf* or infantile. The two words are often confused.

**Je ne sais quoi** – 'I don't know what'. An indefinable quality, an ineffable thingy, a certain whatchemecallit ...

**Jeté** – 'thrown'. Another leap in ballet, in which the dancer springs from one foot to the other. A *grand jeté* is a big one. A *jeté en tournant* is another one of the same, with a turn ...

**Jeton** – a token used to operate a public telephone or slot machine.

**Jeu de paumes/d'esprit** – the phrase *jeu de paumes* is used in English only for the Paris gallery of that name in which, until the establishment of the Quai d'Orsai, the bulk of the Impressionist works were housed. The name means 'game of palms (of the hand)' and refers to what we call Real Tennis which was played on this site.

Now things get complicated, because, of course, Real Tennis is played with racquets, not with the hands, but that is easily enough explained because the game seems to have shared its ancestry with fives and to be descended from an earlier game played with the bare hands. Indeed, the word 'racquet' comes from *raquette*, which in turn is derived from the Arabic *rakhat*, which means the palm of the hand anyhow.

Everything about tennis is etymologically dubious. Start with its name, commonly thought to come from the imperative *Tenetz!* meaning 'Hold!' or 'Receive!' and assumed to have been called by the server as a warning to his opponent. The problem is that we have no record of any such call, though *Accipe!* – 'Accept!' – is recorded. In my humble view, it should be remembered that our source for *Accipe!* is a sixteenth-century Latin one and that the game appears first to have been played in monastic courtyards. It may well be that *Accipe!* was merely the would-be scholarly rendition of a cry already common in the vernacular as *Tenetz*.

Then comes the word 'real', which, many will tell you, is not real at all but the Spanish *real* or the old French *rial* meaning 'royal'. This appears to be untrue. It seems rather that the more immediately obvious explanation, that 'real tennis' was called 'real' to distinguish it from the later 'lawn tennis' is, in fact, the correct one.

Our lawn tennis was not invented until 1873, when one Major Walter Clopton Wingfield invented the game for the amusement of house-party guests at his home in Nantclwyd, Wales. He based the new game and its terminology on 'real tennis' and named it *sphairistike* (ball-game in Greek). This was abbreviated by bright young things to 'sticky'. For a while, then, *ingénues* (*qv*) in light comedies stepped on to the stage with the entrancing words 'Who's for sticky?' It is reputed to have been Stanley Baldwin, of all people, who gently suggested that 'lawn tennis' might catch on rather more easily. Sadly, whoever it was proved right.

A *jeu d'esprit* is literally a game of the spirit or of the wit, so a spontaneous witticism, playful joke or conceit or a short essay, poem, song or other humorous literary work.

**Jeunesse dorée** – literally 'gilded youth', and often so rendered. Wealthy and gifted young people. 'Golden lads and girls all must/As chimney-sweepers, come to dust,' says Shakespeare. Even he proved the point.

**Joie de vivre** – 'joy of living', vivacity, verve, high spirits. The most attractive quality when genuine, the most wearisome when feigned.

**Jolie laide** – you see, here's another example of why Pumphrey and I just could not work together. He wrote 'happy hooker' next to this entry, which is offensive and just plain silly. I have just received an 'e' message from the publisher boy to say that, if I really cannot get on with his uncle, I need no longer try. So as soon as Pumphrey returns, therefore, I will gently and politely ask him to leave me to complete the work in scholarly seclusion as befits a book of such seriousness. The components of this phrase are *jolie* or 'pretty' and *laide*, which is 'ugly', so a sort of woman far more frequently found in France than in England who, although ill-favoured in terms of symmetry, classically balanced features and the like, yet contrives to be alluring and enchanting.

**Jujube** – a sweet or *comfit* largely made of gelatin or gum arabic and originally flavoured with syrup of the jujube tree, whose name is derived from the Latin *zizyphon*, which bears date-like fruit whose name this properly is.

**Julienne** – a reference to an unknown Julius, Jules or Julien? Or to the month? I'm afraid that I don't know. The thing, anyhow, is vegetables cut into narrow strips for incorporation in various dishes.

***Laissez-faire/laissez-passer*** – good governments practise a policy of *laissez-faire* (leave to do) or permit individuals and enterprises to do as they will save where it is injurious to others. Bad governments pass laws banning things which are none of their business. *Laissez-faire* also describes the attitude of all good liberal utilitarians, who do not seek to prevent free choices merely because their consequences are personally distasteful. A **laissez-passer** is merely a document or ordinance such as the British passport which requires and requests free passage 'without let or hindrance' from one place to another to its bearer or subject. My official passport is little, red and very unimpressive – a bit like French partridges and a lot of Frenchmen. I keep it in an imposing midnight-blue folder bearing the royal coat of arms in gilt. Well, we can dream, can't we?

**Lamé** – the glistering fabric worn by 1930s and 1940s filmstars is linked to the word 'laminated'. A *lamina* in Latin is a thin sheet or layer of metal, plate, mica or the like, and 'to laminate' is to force such thin plates by rolling or beating into a thicker fabric. *Lamé* was invented in the 1920s, and is a thread coated or encrusted with a metal or metallic substance and so 'laminated'.

**Langouste/langoustine** – great confusion here. The lobster in French is *homard*, the crayfish *écrevisse*. The word 'lobster' seems to be an Anglicised rendering of the Latin *locusta*– the name for the locust and the lobster alike – influenced, probably, by the Old English *loppe*, a spider and maybe, obscurely, by that famous sailor's dish, 'lobscouse', which is thought in turn to come from a dialect word, 'lob' or 'lop', meaning to seethe or wallop. *Langouste* is a Provençal version of the same word, and is commonly used of the spiny lobster, which is not a true lobster at all, while *langoustine* is used of a variety of smaller crustacea, including the crayfish, the Dublin Bay prawn and its cousin the Adriatic *cinghiale del mare*, but does not seem to have a species all its own.

**Langue de chat** – a long, thin, narrow biscuit, named a cat's tongue because of its shape and eaten with liqueurs or fortified wines or used to line a *charlotte*.

**Langue d'oc/langue d'oil** – the *langue d'oc* is the language spoken south of the Loire in mediaeval France, and so called because *oc* was the word for 'yes', whereas northerners used the word *oil* or *oui*. The *langue d'oc* is the basis of today's Provençal dialect with its characteristic twang: '*Angtoinette, mang-je!*' the nanny used to exhort my cousin at the table. The *langue d'oil* is the basis of modern standard French. The Languedoc as a modern region comprises Roussillon, Haute-Loire, Lozère, Ardèche, Gard, Hérault, Aude, Tarn and Haute-Garonne.

**Largesse** – munificence, liberality, generous giving or a generous gift. From Old French *largesse* meaning a bounty, previously from Latin *largus*, meaning plentiful or copious. Quite why we have to use the French ending for our own 'largeness', which comes from precisely the same source, I am not sure. Certainly 'large' has taken on the later sense of 'breadth' in English, but so it has in French.

**Larmoyant** – lachrymose, prone to tearfulness.

**Lavallière** – a rather dashing and elegant sort of tie with a large, loose knot, halfway between the cravat of the Regency and the bootlace variety favoured by our Western marshal and hired gun friends. Also a pendant necklace and, in broadcasting circles, a microphone hung thus. The word once referred to a whole style of clothing, and was named after Françoise Louise de la Baume Le Blanc, Duchesse de La Vallière, mistress to Louis XIV.

**Layette** – Pumphrey, you will be unsurprised to hear, thought that this was a synonym of *banquette*. It really is a relief to know that I will no longer have to cope with such drivel. When my goddaughter Polly was born (her parents gave her some other name, but I can neither pronounce nor remember it), her idiot father set out to buy a thing called 'a travelcot'. The midwife, a woman of sterling sense, simply asked, 'So, do your friends not have drawers?' because, of course, she knew that the lowest drawer in a commode or chest, lined with a sheepskin, makes an infinitely preferable and more secure bed for an infant than any absurd, unwieldy, cumbersome and expensive flatpack construct of netting and padding with sprung joints which snap shut and consume small children and adult fingers. The reason that I mention this is that a *layette*, a set of clothes or equipment for a newborn, somewhat akin to an infantile *trousseau* (*qv*), derives its name from a word meaning 'chest of drawers' which derives its name in turn from *laie*, which simply means 'drawer', so a single drawer can serve for baby, its clothes and its bedding.

**Legerdemain** – conjuring, sleight of hand, dexterity or tricks or artifices requiring these. From *léger*, light, *de main*, of hand. So too, cunning or trickery, traits highly regarded, from wily Odysseus to Jack the Giantkiller, in almost all almost all cultures save the nineteenth and twentieth century British and North American.

**Légume** – in French, *légume* is the generic word for edible vegetables, but in English, rather more specific, legume denotes those vegetables (leguminous) with seedheads or pods containing seeds – various grasses, peas and such. The word comes from the Latin *legere*, to choose or gather, whence we derive college, collect, elect and many others, the reason being that these are vegetables which can readily be harvested by hand.

**Lèse-majesté** – injured or insulted majesty, violation of the sovereign power of the monarch or – or 'and thereby' – the state. This was a crime on the statute books, *crimen laesae maiestatis*, and somehow became adopted in common speech, where it may figuratively refer to any impertinence towards authority. *Lèse* comes from *laedere*, to hit, wound or damage, whence our 'lesion'.

**Le tout...** – 'all of ...', but in a decidedly social sense, so *le tout Londres*. The phrase is more often used in camp mock affectation than for its actual purpose, that it serves with admirable succinctness and efficiency.

**Levade** – in *haute école dressage* (*qv*), rearing as if to strike. A vile vice formalised and encouraged in this equine form of ballet.

**Levée** – there are two sorts of *levée*. One, famously pronounced to rhyme with 'chevvy' in the incomprehensible 'Bye Bye, Miss American Pie', is a man-made embankment intended to prevent a river's flooding or a natural one caused by silting, and so a quay or pier for mooring. The other variety, pronounced as in French, is another instance of Gallic grandiosity (see *déjeuner*) – a sort of royal working breakfast, but without food, at which honoured guests were permitted to witness the King or some other person of distinction arising from bed in the morning, yawning, stretching, crepitating, scratching and the like. This subsequently became a term for any sort of reception at any time of the day (but not generally of the night).

**Lever le rideau** – a justly archaic borrowing, and should you, as I have twice done, encounter such a thing, I trust that you will have about you your critical faculties and the means of expresssing your considered opinions in the form of addled eggs or fruit. On the first occasion, this was graven in whimsical italic on a concert programme. On the second – and surely there is a circle in hell for such people which Dante missed only through a Virgilian oversight – it was at the top of a menu in an expensive restaurant. So expressly and effectively to turn the stomachs of all right-thinking diners before they order must surely speak of deliberate losses for tax. The phrase means 'to raise the curtain'. We have curtain-raisers – and gorge-raisers – of our own.

**Liaison** – *lier* (from *ligare*) is to bind, and this term is properly used of the thickening of sauces by, for example, the use of a *roux* or egg-yolks and of the sauces so bound, which, with the exception of my Hollandaise (which is an emulsion anyhow) tend to remain so bound. In the nineteenth and twentieth centuries, however, the word came to mean, euphemistically and generally inappositely, a connection, usually illicit, between a man and a woman who, if bound, were only temporarily so and in fetters of cowhide, chain or silk. 'We had a brief liaison' does not mean, 'we guzzled a *béchamel*', but 'we fornicated'. Meanwhile, though you might have thought the euphemism unnecessary and the associations unfortunate, business seized upon this word to mean 'communication' or 'association with a view to discussion'. So 'liaison officers' were appointed to create such relationships, and a curious new verb, 'to liaise', sprang up, meaning 'to talk' or, if there is an expense account involved, 'to get drunk'.

**Limaçon** – a spiral staircase, snail-shell or similar whorled construct, whence springs a discussion worthy of general participation. Thanks to email, the long-neglected @ symbol has suddenly risen to prominence, and its once pristine key on the Remington is now one of the brownest on the computer keyboard, yet English, most blessed, richest and most poetic of tongues, has no word for it save 'the at sign'.

I am grateful to Martha Barnette in her *Dog Days and Dandelions* for raising this issue in a delightful essay on the word 'cochlea', which is, of course, an anatomical term relating to the snail-like cavity within the ear, and is so called because the Greek *kocklia* is generic term for whelks, winkles and other invertebrates with spiral shells. Ms Barnette points out that the word for snail doubles with that for @ in Korean and Esperanto, while Israelis refer to the symbol, charmingly, as a *strudel*. In Hungarian, she says, the @ is a maggot, in Russian a little dog and in Greek a duckling. In German, Dutch, Serbo-Croat and Bulgarian, it is a monkey, while the Taiwanese see it as a little mouse and some Scandinavians as a cat. The Danes and Swedes mysteriously see it as a *snabel a*, or 'elephant's trunk a'. Personally, I rather favour *strudel*, not merely because of its appositeness but because the word and the pastry have been internationally adopted, but we really cannot continue with that ugly and frequently confusing 'at sign'. Whichever term you favour, please use it constantly, and linguistic natural selection will take its course. Maybe it should be a *limaçon*?

PAR AVION

**Lingerie** – euphemism for ladies', or, at least, women's, underwear, though I can think of little which less needs a euphemism. For some unfathomable reason, this is frequently pronounced 'long-je-ray' by uneducated British persons. These are the same people who habitually pronounce 'plastic' and 'elastic' with long 'a's and call a vase a 'vawz', presumably in the belief that this is the way in which refined French people contort their mouths in speaking.

*Lingerie*, of course, comes from *linge*, linen, so actually means 'linen stuff', from the Latin *linum*, flax. *Lingerie*, however, is rarely linen. The term 'underwear' now seems acceptable for natural fibres, while *lingerie* is reserved for frills, flounces and furbelows in slithery man-made fabrics, lace and, of course, silk.

**Locale** – a totally absurd word, supposedly meaning 'place' or 'locality'. The absurdity is compounded by the facts not only that we possess these words but that the French word denoting 'place' or 'premises' is *local*, and that the truly odious people who use this word have added the 'e' just to demonstrate that they are using a French term and are therefore delicate and discerning. In fact, they demonstrate that their vocation is the wrapping of confectionery and that their brains and taste are negligible.

**Longueur** – a *longueur* is a turbid, tedious passage of writing, music, drama etc., sometimes, like a holding pool on a salmon fishery, deep, slow and offering almost no prospect of sport but necessary to the health of the sprightlier whole; more frequently indicative of the author's self-importance and self-indulgence and canalising the entire work, as in, say, John Fowles.

**Lorgnette** – a *lorgnette* (*lorgnettes* is also acceptable for the same thing) is a splendid thing, an indispensable optical aid and a supremely effective, sometimes deadly weapon. I own three of these things, inherited from my late mother, who could drive shiftless tradesmen into early retirement, quell armed revolution, render hot-blooded suitors impotent for months and generally restore society to order with a mere click of the apparatus and a raising of the eyebrows. A *lorgnette* is a pair of eyeglasses, generally highly ornamented and wrought in precious metals, enamel and jewels, usually released by a spring-action mechanism to enable the user to see clearer and the victim the better to relearn his or her rightful station in life.

**Louche** – in its English usage, *louche* means disreputable, vulgar, seamy or sleazy. When used of a political party or a doctor, say, it is invariably derogatory. When used of a cocktail bar or a glamour model, however, it may be, albeit perversely, mildly approving, so 'it (or she) has a certain rather *louche* charm ...' This is a long way from the word's origin, which is the Latin *lusca* meaning one-eyed. Thence, in its French form, it came to mean 'cross-eyed' or 'squinting', and so, in the nineteenth century, indecent or disreputable.

**Luge** – toboggan, or, rather, tea tray on runners on which to slither down snowy hills. Origin unknown. Two-man luge is unquestionably the most purposeless and, where not purposeless, deviant sport which I have ever witnessed. If truly needful, it should surely be performed only in the privacy of one's own bathroom.

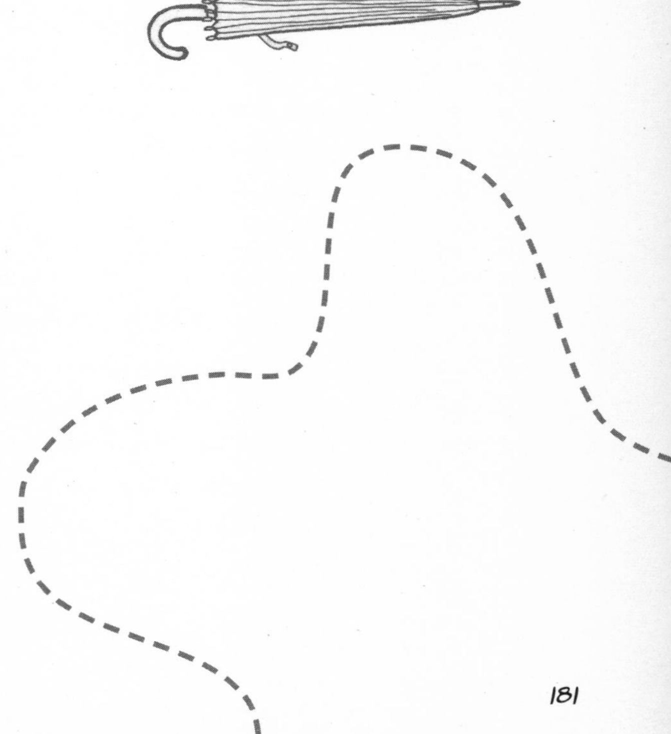

***Macédoine*** – an assortment of fruit or, more usually, vegetables, cut small or diced to be served as a side-dish in its own right or as a constituent of soups or stews etc. Said to be a reference to the diversity of peoples in the Macedonian empire or army of Alexander the Great. Frequently today used figuratively and mildly camply for any motley mixture or *tutti frutti* of people or things.

***Mâche*** – lamb's lettuce is abundant in British hedgerows and available for free. By the time that it is called *mâche*, however, it is available only at huge expense in city delicatessens.

**Madame** – madam, my lady, Mrs, and used as such a form of address by pretentious servitors when not acquainted with a patroness's name or title. Also frequently substituted for 'madam' for the proprietress of a brothel. From *ma (mea) dame (domina)*.

**Mademoiselle** – miss. Association with generations of governesses has afforded this form of address a primness in English which it does not in fact and in itself possess and which would have surprised Mademoiselle from Armentiers, to whom millions of Britons have melodiously addressed the question 'Parlez-vous?' 'Demoiselle', of course, is none other but our own 'damsel', originally *domnicella*, a diminutive of *domina*, a lady or mistress of a household.

**Maison clos** – a 'closed house' or brothel.

**Maison de passe** – a house or, more commonly, a flat to which prostitutes can take clients for brief, 'hotsheeting' encounters.

**Maisonette** – heaven knows. Literally 'a little house', this is another bit of estate-agent speak, now denoting any self-contained unit, usually but not always on more than one floor, within a larger house. So a flat with a window-box.

**Maître/maître d'/cher maître** – where lawyers in Britain are habitually addressed as 'Oy, bloodsucker!' or 'Bill Matey' (as in, 'If you think I'm paying that …', the French afford them the respectful honorific, *maître* or 'master'. More aptly, the *maître d'*, or *maître d'hotel* (master of the house) is a head waiter or, today in an age of gratuitous positions of authority, a restaurant manager. The term was originally identical to our own 'steward', 'butler' or 'factor', denoting the person charged with the smooth running of the domestic staff of a great house. *Cher maître* is the entirely proper form of address used to great writers, conductors and other artists. Pumphrey has consistently neglected to address me as such.

**Malade imaginaire** – oh, dear. It is quite sweet. Pumphrey has left me a scrawled note here, 'Imaginary duck. Suppose the Frogs have these like our children have imaginary friends. Anyhow, that gloomy old Norwegian chappy wrote a play about one. Very odd. Long dark nights, I suppose, and cheese that tastes like saddle soap. You can understand it'. It took me really quite a while to realise what my former colleague was talking about, but at last I realised that he referred to Ibsen's *The Wild Duck*, which does indeed deal with a man who believes that he has a duck in his attic rooms. In fact, of course, the phrase *malade imaginaire* has nothing whatever to do with ducks, and I really need a lie-down. *Malade* means 'sick', from the Latin *male habitus*, meaning 'in poor condition', so a *malade imaginaire* is a hypochondriac or one with a fictitious sickness, like most people's grandmothers. The term was indeed made famous by a playwright, but in this case Molière, whose comedy of this name was first produced in 1673.

**Maladroit** – undexterous, clumsy (see *gauche* above).

**Malapropos** – (see *à-propos* above). Inopportune, inappropriate, not *apropos*. So, as Pumphrey wrote to me in a letter from Aberfeldy today, '*Sans doute* you think my interventions *malapropos* as crepitations at a Papal lying-in-state …' This word, of course, gives its name to the absurd Mrs Malaprop who, in a characteristic lower-class bid at sesquipedelianism and grandiloquence where monosyllabic simplicity would have sufficed, frequently mistook her words.

**Mal de mer** – sea-sickness. I have heard it suggested that our 'marmalade' owes its name to *mer* (or *mare*, sea) and *malade*, implying that the virtues of preserved oranges in the prevention of scurvy might have been recognised as early as the 1520s when the word first entered our language. Alas, this delightful theory is unfounded. The word comes to us from the Portuguese *marmelo* meaning quince (a strange etymology, this, for *marmelo* appears to come from *mellis*, honey, and *melon*, *malus*, apple, implying that the bitter quince was thought of as a 'honey-apple', which seems most unlikely. Still, there it is.

**Mal élevé/e** – ill-mannered, badly brought up. See *bien élevé/e*.

**Mal entendu** – misheard, misunderstood. Often used as a noun, as in, 'I believe that the whole dispute was a result of a single *mal entendu*'.

**Malgré lui** – despite himself. Molière wrote a play called *Le Médecin Malgré Lui*, or 'The Doctor Despite Himself', and we might say, 'Loneliness and well-meaning if misplaced concern for morale cause him to make puerile jokes *malgré lui*'.

**MALPT** – a really rather jolly way of wishing someone exceptionally good luck, this is an acronym for *Merde à la puissance treize*, or 'shit to the power of thirteen.' Very strange.

**Mange-tout** – 'eat all' – a sugar or snap pea, whose pods are extremely tender in texture and delicate in flavour, whence the name. These were inordinately fashionable in the seventeenth century, though the people of Islington and other suburbs convinced themselves that they had invented them in the late twentieth.

**Mannequin** – an artist's hinged human figurine or a clothes dummy, animate or inanimate. Another case of an unnecessary repeated borrowing. We had 'manikin' for a jointed human figure, as used by artists, back in the sixteenth century. The word came to us direct from the Dutch *manneken*, meaning 'little man', and is occasionally used in English folk tales and insults to mean just this. The French too had taken this word from the Low Countries, and naturally rendered it *mannequin*. It was in the eighteenth century that, no doubt considering Dutch and English altogether too mundane, the usual suspects, the artistic and fashionable worlds, disdaining the previous import, looked across the Channel and came back with the excitingly different, outstandingly sophisticated *mannequin* – exactly the same word but satisfyingly harder to spell or pronounce correctly.

**Manqué/e** – literally 'missed' or 'lacked', used of something which might have been but which never came into being. So 'she is a musician *manquée*' or 'They are lovers *manqués*'. I see that Pumphrey has described a certain popular singer as 'a manky monkey *manqué*', which is really quite good, for him.

**Maquillage/maquiller** – make-up, noun and verb respectively, from *masquiller* to stain, from *mascurer* to darken, related to the Spanish *máscara*, soot, mask, which springs from the same root as the Italian *maschera*, a mask. So all the meanings of mask, soot, stain, darken and mascara are retained and contained in the one root, which is the Latin *masca*, meaning mask, spectre or nightmare …

**Maquis** – dense, scrubby undergrowth, particularly of Corsica where the bandits come from, and hence the French Resistance during the Second World War, most of whose heroic members were promptly executed as collaborators by collaborators (now generally mayors, EU Commissioners and the like), who had to get rid of them before the Allies arrived.

**Mariage blanc** – 'white marriage' as opposed to, or distinct from, a white wedding. A *mariage blanc* is what we assume 'lavender marriages' (*mariages de convenance* (*qv*) between homosexuals) to be – that is, unconsummated.

**Mariage de convenance** – a marriage of convenience. An altogether splendid institution.

**Mari complaisant** – a wise husband whose worth is above rubies, who tolerates and tacitly colludes in his wife's adulteries, usually after she has provided him with the statutory 'heir and a spare', thus assuring social stability and tranquillity.

**Matelot** – sailor. Whimsical on the lips of civilians, but normal parlance in the British Royal Navy. This is of course the French word for 'sailor', from the Dutch *mattenoot*, 'bed companion', because sailors had to share hammocks. Certainly in the case of buccaneers, they shared a deal more besides. They entered into a quasi-official sexual relationship called *matelotage*, and, when fortunate enough to take a woman on board, shared her too. It seems, then, that Pumphrey's scurrilous ditty about the good ship named *Venus*, whose cabin-boy, named Nipper, was thought to be 'a ripper' – '*They filled his arse/With broken glass/And circumcised the skipper*', is not, after all, so far from the truth, though why he has to sing about anything so distasteful eludes me. It is thought that 'mate', as in 'bosun's mate' may be derived from *matelot*, though, if this be the case, the word must have been conflated with the far more ancient 'mate' meaning 'fellow' or 'partner'.

## Mauvais quart d'heure

– 'bad quarter of an hour'. I can find no reference to this earlier than the delightful, profligate, happy Giacomo Rossini's witty, astute comment regarding Wagner's *Ring* cycle: '*Il y a des beaux moments, mais des mauvais quarts d'heure*' – 'there are some fine moments, but some bad quarter-hours' (see *longueur*, above). Although this phrase is sometimes now used literally, simply to denote unenjoyable but brief periods, this merely sounds, and is, gratuitously pretentious. The allusion to Rossini's *bon mot* (*qv*) with its implication of those barely-worth-it *beaux moments* (the game of football supplies an excellent opportunity for the use of this phrase) is the sole justification for its use.

**Mêlée** – a skirmish or hand-to-hand fight, often confused and distinguished from a more orderly and, generally, larger battle. Curious that this, which comes from *mêler (mesler)* to mix, whence meddle, *mélange* and meld, should be echoed in the modern usage, 'to mix it', meaning to brawl.

**Ménage à trois** – *Ménage* comes from the Latin *mansio*, whence too the Scottish manse and our mansion, and previously from *manere*, to stay or abide, and means a household. A *ménage à trois* is therefore a household of three, commonly a man with a wife and a mistress, and can work very nicely if one of the women knows her place and is happy to help with the children, horses etc. as well as in bed. It also happens that a husband and wife may invite her lover to join them in their *ménage*, which can be very tiring.

**Menu sans prix** – another incoherent Pumphreyism. He has here written, 'I say, you chaps are transsexuals!' Of course, a *menu sans prix* is a menu without prices, and is customarily handed to the lady or to guests at a restaurant in order to obviate embarrassment when ordering.

**Merde** – shit. *Le mot de Cambronne*. Nothing illustrates better the ambivalence in French self-perception than this word. The French talk beautiful wars where others fight ugly ones. Their literature is crammed full of high-flown references to *la gloire* and *l'honneur*, but they are far too busy writing this stuff to get out there where it is distastefully noisy and often dangerous, so they generally surrender to save time.

Now, when Pierre Jacques, Baron de Cambronne, was called upon to surrender to Colonel Halkett at Waterloo, he is meant to have said, '*La Garde meurt, mais il ne se rend pas*,' or 'The Guards die, but they do not surrender.' Stirring stuff, but Cambronne himself let the side down, not only by surviving, but by denying that he had ever spoken these words. He claimed rather that he had in fact replied, '*Merde*,' which is altogether more soldierly as we in Britain understand the word. Either way, he and his Guards promptly thereafter surrendered (the *Oxford Dictionary of Quotations* somehow omits the 'Er, actually, on second thoughts ...' following his defiant words or word) so that they could write the truth for posterity in peace.

**Mésalliance** – a bad or misguided marriage or other alliance made between two ill-suited persons. So the poet, summarising Henry James's *Portrait of a Lady*, tells us of Isabel Archer, 'She still kept her skirt on/When Baron Warburton/Proposed that she carry his Hons;/But with one Osmond, Gilbert,/A terrible pill but/Refined, she made *mésalliance*.'

**Méthode champenoise** – the method whereby naturally sparkling wines, notably champagne, are made and stored by allowing the final fermentation to take place within the bottle. This is claimed by the French as one of their great innovations. Alas, not so. This method requires sturdy glass bottles, and such glass was unknown in France in 1668 when Dom Pierre Pérignon arrived at the Benedictine Abbey of Hautvillers and accidentally discovered how to make his red wine sparkle. It was, however, common in Britain because we had abundant coal with which to heat our glass to very high temperatures, and it was the cider-makers who recorded this method at the Royal Society a full half-century before the French applied it to wine. Not that I wish to encourage Pumphreyesque triumphalism or anything, but one does like to be accurate.

**Métier** – trade, craft or, by extension, any form of work for which a particular aptitude is shown. From the Latin *ministerium*, service or office. So we have no need of *métier* in its literal sense, since 'job' or 'trade' will serve admirably, but it is useful in contradistinction, as in, 'He earned his living as a chicken-sexer, but his true *métier* was that of a bullfighter.'

**Mezzanine** – obviously an Italian word, from *mezza/mezzana*, half or middling, Latin *media/mediana*, medium, but taken into English from the French to mean an extra floor or storey squeezed in between two others, generally between the ground floor and the basement or the ground floor and the former first floor.

**Midinette** – an enchanting word for a shop-girl, frequently a milliner's assistant, thought to be taken from *midi*, midday, and *dinette*, a light dinner, and to refer to the dietary habits of such women. Frankly, I suspect this to be a peculiarly English and improbably proper explanation, for *midinettes* enjoyed the same reputation as English dollymops – normal girls of not exactly easy but none too difficult virtue who might just be persuaded to give a personable and generous young fellow a good time.

**Mignonne** – I give this only in its feminine form, since it is generally only thus that the word is used today. The word means 'sweet, delicate, pretty, charming', and can be used as an endearment in its own right – *ma mignonne* …'

**Migraine** – originally from the Greek *hemi* (half) *kranion* (skull). A mighty headache. We have the form 'megrim' meaning melancholy, alas now rarely used.

**Mirage** – an optical illusion, usually the phantasm of water, buildings or vegetation seen through heat-haze, particularly in the desert. Sometimes this is illusion, sometimes the reflection of a distant but actual object. From *se mirer*, to look at one's reflection, from the Latin *mirare*, to wonder at, whence miracle, admire, Miranda (she upon whom one should gaze) etc.

**Mise au point/en scène/en place** – a *mise au point* is the elucidation of an otherwise confused or unclear subject of discussion or thought.

The *mise en scène* of a play or film is the setting, scenery, properties, costumes etc., the dramatic realisation on the stage or set of the words on the page. It has nothing to do with rodents or rivers, thank you, Pumphrey. The *mise en place* is the putting in place, preparation and assemblage of ingredients for cooking in the kitchen or, indeed, in other arts and crafts – what we would call 'prepping'.

**Modiste** – a frock-designer, seamstress or milliner with very outdated pretensions.

**Moi?** – a mock-modest protestation made popular by the belligerent and amorous Muppet Miss Piggy who would object, 'Aggressive? *Moi?*' or 'Beautiful? *Moi?*' or some such. This became a catchphrase, and the single word is now widely used after epithets, accusing or complimentary.

**Moiré** – watered, watery, shimmery, cloudy, as of watered or *moiré* silk. It might be said, with some difficulty, that a *mirage* (*qv*) is an image *moiré* by the rising heat.

**Mondaine** – see **Demi-mondaine**.

**Monstre sacré** – literally holy or sacred monster. A sort of adult *enfant terrible*, a notable, striking, influential, respected and often an eccentric figure in a particular field.

**Montage** – a judicious assemblage of individual articles or images to create an effect. This may be as in a still life, where objects are grouped, or in film or photography, where shots or sequences are thus combined in their own sequence or melded to create one composite image, emotional effect or shorthand narrative.

**Morceau** – a morsel, gobbet or tidbit of music or literature. Totally superfluous borrowing assumed to afford artistic credibility simply on the grounds of the evident stupidity and poor taste of the speaker in using a weary foreign word where English has countless alternatives and imagination would supply many more.

**Motif** – a theme or principal or recurrent idea in music, argument etc. 'Motif' and 'motive' both existed in Middle English, initially meaning a proposition or premise, then coming to mean a cause of action or thought (from *movere*, to move).

**Mot juste** – 'Person called Maureen, liquidised?' I now know Pumphrey's conceits well enough to recognise that this note must have been written very late at night, with a large amount of whisky taken. *Le mot juste* is the perfect or apt word or phrase for a concept or thing.

**Mouton enragé** – enraged sheep. A meek or placid person who is pushed too far and suddenly becomes fierce or, at least, petulant. A worm who has turned.

**Naïf/naive** – innocent, artless, unsophisticated or, when used pejoratively, ignorant. From the Latin *nativus*, native or rustic, with all the associations at once of the admirably unspoiled and of the irritatingly callow (whose root word, incidentally, means 'bald').

**Nécessaire** – a little case fitted to contain scissors, tweezers, earpicks and other ladies' accoutrements.

**Négligée** – a loose, generally diaphanous garment, akin to a dressing gown but often trimmed with frippery frills, flounces and bits of dead beasts, worn by women when supposedly relaxing but often when intent upon seduction. The name often baffles, since it is so clearly a feminine past participle meaning 'neglected', from the verb *négliger*, and it is plain that a woman donning such a garment intends to be anything but. The explanation lies in the (admittedly *simplex munditiis*) informality and carelessness of the attire – in the words of Violet Bick in *It's a Wonderful Life*, 'Oh, this old thing? Why, I only wear it when I don't care how I look!'

**Niche** – a hollowed-out nook or recess in a wall, and so, by extension, a position well suited to a person's talents or predispositions. From *nicher*, to nest and Italian *nicchia*, nook and *nicchio*, a seashell. You see how easily and rapidly the scholarship flows when I am left alone to concentrate without interruptions, silliness and intemperate opinions? I can have no doubt but that this is, as it were, my niche, just with the books and Bach and the canary. Pumphrey returns tomorrow. I will have to be firm.

**Noblesse/noblesse oblige** – *noblesse* is used a trifle more precisely in French than in modern English, perhaps because the thing itself is so rare in France since all those ghastly middle-class pseuds behaved so disgracefully at the end of the eighteenth century. They would have been teachers today, of course – beards, anoraks, vegetarianism, noxious spray-on deodorants, resentment disguised as revisionist history and doctrinaire droolings as considered opinions – mass murderers every one, if given half a chance, like all brainless puritans … Anyhow, yes. *Noblesse* actually means 'nobility' as a class or grouping distinguished from others by an inherited rank once associated with specific lands and so specific responsibilities. And it is these responsibilities which the dictum *noblesse oblige* asserts – the principle that noble birth entails obligations quite as great as those today performed inadequately by so-called 'Welfare States', which assume power by presuming – and generally failing – to assume responsibilities.

PAR AVION

## Nom de guerre/de plume

– a *nom de guerre* is the assumed name under which a mercenary or other person who wishes to retain anonymity or apparent neutrality enrols and serves in an armed force. A *nom de plume* is similarly an assumed name under which an author publishes his or her work – a pen name, from *nom*, name, *de*, of and *guerre* and *plume*, respectively war and pen. The phrase *nom de guerre* is now used figuratively for many a pseudonym used in other curious enterprises, such as acting, sexual adventures etc.

**Nonchalant/nonchalance** – *chaloir* is an interesting word which means at once to care and to be warm. It is derived, of course, from the Latin *calere*, which means at once to be warm or heated and to be emotionally stirred, from which root we take 'calorie', 'cauldron' and the like. To be *non-chalant*, therefore, is not to care or to be indifferent. The meaning has shifted slightly, however, to resemble that of 'cool' – that is, elegantly lackadaisical rather than necessarily unfeeling.

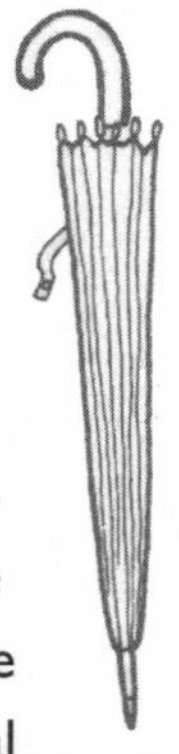

**Nonpareil** – without peer, unrivalled, or, as a noun, one considered to be so. This word has been used in English since the fifteenth century.

**Nostalgie de la boue** – oh, dear. I have here a note saying, 'Happy memories of sudden surprises'. In fact, 'nostalgia for mud', or a perverse longing for indignity, grime and depravity. This is something that we find a deal of in Russian literature, where it appears to have been a culturally ingrained psychosis, but the phrase became current at the end of the nineteenth century, where it was considered a desirable trait in the artist. Baudelaire cultivated it, but one or two others, notably the English poet Francis Thompson, appeared to find it a compulsion. Thompson, a gentleman and scholar, lived on the streets until he won literary success, briefly attempted to 'clean up his act' and then voluntarily returned to his former life of degradation.

**Nous autres** – 'we others'. A snobbish phrase closely akin to the English 'PLU' (People Like Us) and encapsulated, slightly more charmingly, in one of Pumphrey's favourite toasts, 'Here's to us, those like us …' to which the unison rejoinder is, 'Damned few.'

**Nouveau pauvre/nouveau riche** – *nouveau pauvre* or 'newly poor' is the condition of all of us who may claim to be cultured, educated and well-mannered today, with the happy exception of those born poor. The phrase is modelled, however, on *nouveau riche* or 'newly rich', the condition, it seems, of almost everyone else. The *nouveau pauvre* are not readily distinguished in that they consider their financial wellbeing to be no one's business but their own. The *nouveau riche*, however, are notable for their ostentatious displays of wealth. They are frequently referred to simply as *nouveaux*. They are universally despised save by their own kind.

**Nouvelle cuisine** – a movement of the 1970s which, like punk, had few inherent merits but none the less left a salutary influence when once it had passed away. The thing itself was largely manifest in overpriced, minuscule items of millinery on a diner's plate – a crown consisting in a solitary sweetbread, a plume of wafer-thin baked Parmesan, a brim of wilted spinach, a veil of Sauternes, beaded with diced carrots or some such – all 'garnished' with irrelevant things such as strawberries and mangoes. The stress on fresh and healthy ingredients, however, on the composition of a plate as an adventure in scents, savours and textures rather than as a selection of bland, unrelated ingredients uniformly blanketed in sauce, has happily survived its misfortunate origins.

**Nuance** – an enchanting word, meaning a shade or subtle shift of meaning, colour etc. Of course, the source is the same as that for the delicious *nuage*, cloud (and I have heard really quite respectable and sensible Britons, when asked if they favour milk in their coffee, reply, 'just a *nuage*, please,'), which is *nuer*, to shade, originally from Latin *nubes*, cloud, and *obnubere*, to veil.

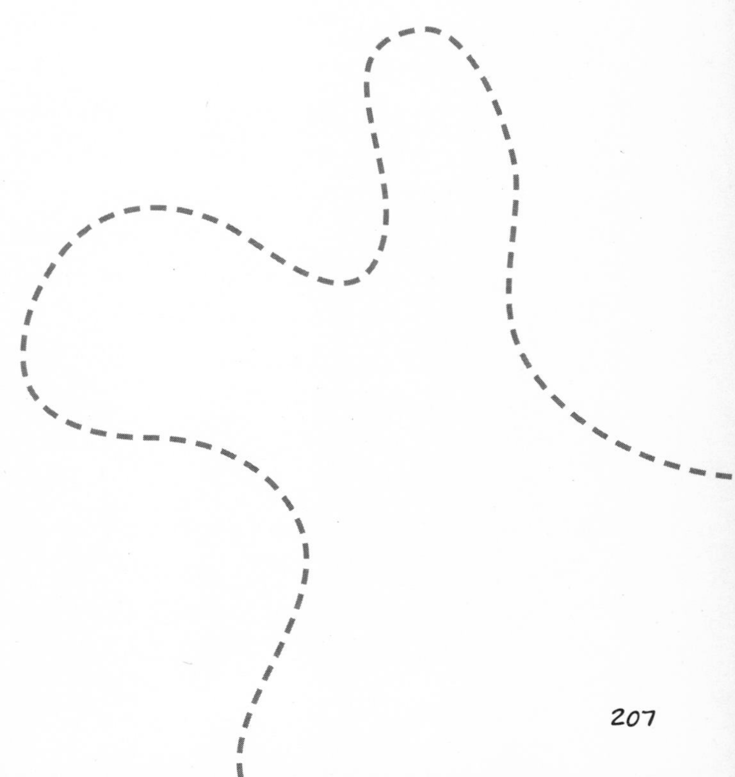

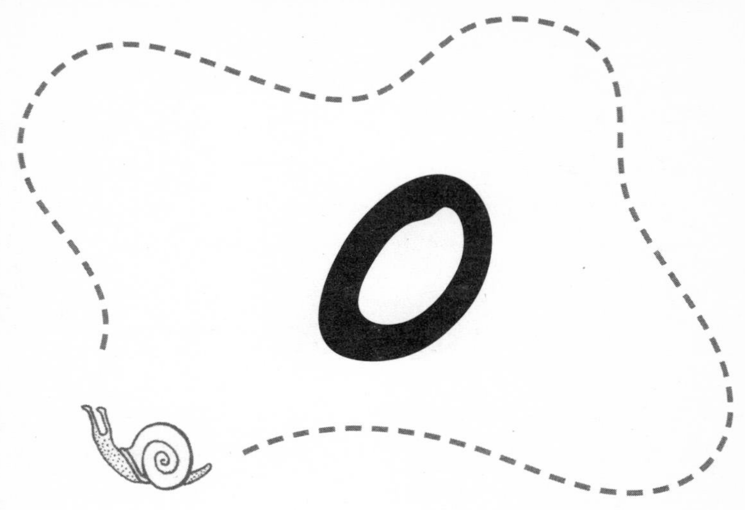


***Objet d'art/de vertu*** – a brave attempt to distinguish one sort of *bric-à-brac* (*qv*) from others and thereby to justify higher prices and greater pride in possession. If we presumed to describe a limited-edition Taiwanese figurine of a shepherd girl named Mabellyne (with flower-enravelled crook, constipated expression and King Charles spaniel) as 'an object of art', we would properly be derided. As an *objet d'art*, however, it might pass unchallenged. This is not to say that there are not ornamental items of glass, porcelain, enamel and the like which may reasonably be described as 'art', but the claims of most to this description would generally be the subject of debate. As to *objets de vertu*, these are articles which have renounced even the implausible claim to be art and fall back rather on their associations with historic figures or the craft with which they were wrought, both of which can rightly be considered 'virtues' .

**Odalisque** – artists liked to portray *odalisques,* in that this identification, purporting to be foreign, exotic and possibly historic, allowed them to paint their girlfriends naked and in provocative poses and to use no props beyond a judiciously placed scrap of silk and an Oriental carpet. An *odalisque* purports to be a concubine in an Oriental seraglio or harem, and the word comes from the Turkish meaning 'chamber-person', from *oda*, chamber.

**Oeil de boeuf** – ox-eye or bull's eye. A round window.

**Oeuvre** – 'a work' of art or, more commonly, the corpus or totality of an artist's work.

**Oubliette** – a cellar, dungeon or hiding place accessible only through a trap-door. From *oublier*, to forget, whether because such places and their contents were frequently forgotten or, more probably, because that was the rarely fulfilled intention of their constructors, is uncertain.

**Oyez/oyes** – I hesitate to include this word, because it is properly Anglo-Norman and has therefore been part of English for as long as of French, and all its letters should therefore be pronounced. This is the cry of the court officer and town-crier, demanding or commanding attention. It is, of course, the imperative plural of *ouïr*, to hear, from the Latin *audire* and so simply means 'Hear!' or 'Listen!'

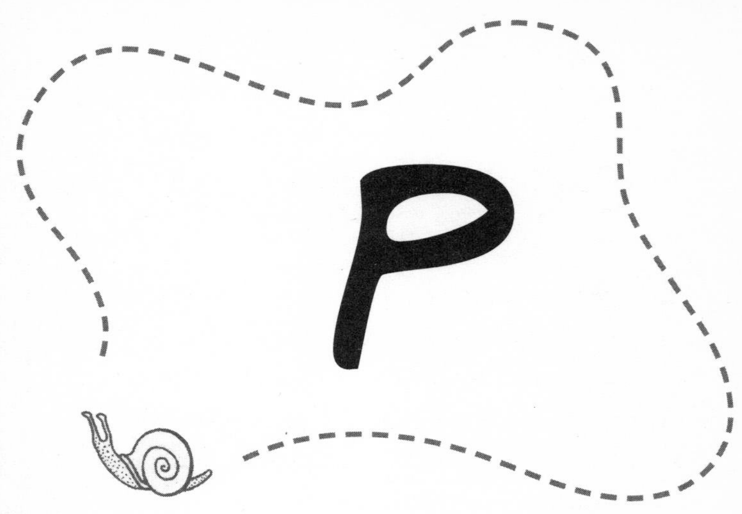


**Palais, palais de danse** – is it significant, I wonder, that I start on 'P' just as Pumphrey returns, dishevelled and tartan-eyed, having endured a hellish night on the sleeper so that I could not even consider broaching the subject of his continued residence here until he had gone upstairs for a few hours' sleep and a scrub-up? It really is very hard. He brought me a bolt of Harris tweed from Brora and a litre of Laphroaig. What can one do, pray, with such a man? Anyhow, a *palais* is, of course, a palace, which takes its name from the Palatine Hill in Rome, where the Emperor Augustus had his magnificent home and the Emperor Nero his absurdly opulent one. Proceeding, then, from the ridiculous to the ridiculous, with a large number of sublimities in between, we arrive at the *palais de danse*, frequently referred to as the *palais* or 'pally', which is, of course, a dance-hall

**Panache** – a *panache* is a plume or crest of feathers, as worn by grebes and chivalric knights. The origin of this word appears, somewhat improbably, to be the Latin *pinna*, a peak, which is thought to derive in turn from *penna*, a feather. All very strange and circular. Anyhow, today the word denotes the flamboyance and gallantry of the knight or courtier who sported such a thing.

**Panier de crabes** – 'basket of crabs'. A most expressive phrase describing a free-for-all fight or competition.

**Panperdy** – from *pain perdu* or 'lost bread'. What the Americans call 'eggy-bread', though seventeenth century originals of panperdy more closely resemble omelettes or custards in which the impregnated bread truly is lost in the finished dish. Now making a welcome comeback but, incredibly, usually referred to as … *pain perdu* …

**Papier mâché** – 'chewed paper'. The French word *mâcher*, to chew, comes from the Latin *masticare*. *Papier mâché* is generally a hideous, knobbly substance of paper worked with glue which looks as though it has indeed been partially chewed before ingestion and regurgitation. Children work it into curiously poignant – even tragic – models of their dogs or parents, or pink and purple photograph frames which cause people to weep late at night. In Victorian times, however, this substance was made into highly polished and beautifully decorated trays and furniture in imitation of lacquer. It is all too sad to bear thinking about, really.

**Par excellence** – Pumphrey just came down in his dressing gown, all bleary-eyed and spiky-haired and swinging in the breeze, and has suggested that this must be a golf term meaning 'albatross'. Really, one does not know how that extraordinary brain works! I have told him that I am coping, thank you, and that he must return to bed. The term actually means, 'above all other exemplars' or 'supremely'.

**Par exemple** – ridiculous phrase precisely meaning 'for example' in the same number of syllables.

**Parfaits** – a *parfait* ('perfect') is a layered ice-cream made in a lined mould, unless you are American, in which case it is an ice-cream with fruit, sauce and cream – what we in Europe would call a *coupe* or a 'sundae'. Just to compound the absurdity of gastro-speak, the word 'sundae' is actually derived from the English word 'Sunday' (one American parlour owner served such concoctions only on that day), but this was obviously too mundane a word for gastronomic use, and, within a few years, the term had returned to the US – if, indeed, it ever went away – in its improbable, exotic, pseudo-French form.

**Parquet** – is inlaid wooden flooring, or, more commonly today, veneer imitating such. A curious derivation, this: *parquet* is a little *parc* or park, or, perhaps, an enclosed section of a park. Your guess is as good as mine as to how the word made the leap from its original, outside meaning to its modern, inside one. Could it be that the flooring was thought to resemble a maze or knot-garden, or that dance-floors or bandstands with such flooring were erected in parks?

**Parterre** – *par terre* means on the ground, but the English usage of the compound word denotes a level space, often sunken, which is made up of a patterned arrangement of flowerbeds or ornamental vegetable beds.

**Parti pris** – a *parti* is a side or faction in a match or contest (hence 'partisan'). A *parti pris* is therefore a view or a position taken before an argument, a prejudice or bias, while one described as *parti pris* is so prejudiced.

**Partouze** – a jolly, playful event at which guests take off their clothes and frolic indiscriminately with one another – an orgy, I suppose we should call it. These happen a lot in Paris, but they also happen a lot just down the road from here. It is just that we prefer to ascribe such things to the French.

**Parvenu/e** – past participle of *parvenir* – to arrive – so one who has arrived, unlike an *arriviste* (*qv*) who thinks that he or she has done so or hopes shortly to do so. Of course, one who is aware of having 'arrived' plainly has not, which is the implication of the word.

**Passé** – out of date, past one's sell-by date, outmoded.

**Passe-partout** – 'pass everywhere'. The name of Phileas Fogg's valet and travelling companion comes from the French word for a skeleton key. Any permit or pass permitting such ubiquitous wandering may also be thus described. Also a sort of adhesive tape used in framing photographs.

**Pastiche** – a work in the style of, but not necessarily parodying, another author, artisan or artist, or a composite of portions of such works combined to create a specific effect. Originally from the Italian *pasticcio*, which means a medley but is also the term for a sweet pastry.

**Pâtisserie/pâtissier/ère** – a *pâtissier/ère* is a pastry-cook, which is as different from a normal cook as a cart-horse from a pony. They have nothing whatever to say to one another, perform entirely different functions and possess entirely different skills. They therefore have profound and proper respect for one another. A pâtisserie is a pâtissier's shop, while pâtisserie is his or her craft or produce.

**Patois** – local dialect, pidgin or jargon, from Old French *patoier*, to handle clumsily or roughly, which comes in turn from *patte*, a paw. Interesting, that …

**Patron** – fully Anglicised since the fourteenth century for most of its meanings – patron of the arts, patron saint, sponsor of talent or ambition, customer of a retail outlet or tavern etc., yet mysteriously retaining its French pronunciation when used to mean the proprietor of a French *auberge*, restaurant, brothel etc., so that a patron of such an establishment may complain to the *patron*. Pure perversity. The word comes to us, of course, from *pater*, father, whence *patronus*, defender or advocate.

**Paysan/paysanne** – a country person, especially one who works the land. Where the word 'peasant' has become, in this nation of urban *arrivistes* (*qv*), an insult, in France it still denotes a member of the noblest calling and possibly the highest culture known to man.

**Péage** – often thought to be related to *payer* or even, via infelicitous Franglais, our own 'pay', but in fact meaning 'footage' (and so 'mileage'), from the

Latin *pes*, a foot, *péage* is a toll exacted for passing along a road or through a specific territory.

**Peignoir** – a loose dressing gown for a woman. This comes from *peigner* Latin *pectinare*), to comb (nothing to do with pectin, by the way, which comes from the Greek *pektos*, congealed), because the original *peignoir* was a garment worn over the shoulders while the hair was combed, like those capes hairdressers use to this day.

**Penchant** – one of those usages which mirrors our own. A *penchant* for something is a leaning or inclination towards it, and lo! *pencher* is to lean or to incline. Of course, if you are prone to do something, you would think that this denoted an even greater inclination, whereas it actually indicates only an occasional tendency or penchant.

**Pension** – a boarding house or boarding school at which a regular rent or fee is paid for residence, from the Latin *pensio*, rent, in turn from *pendere*, to weigh (so interesting to consider that *pendere* also gave us *penser* and pensive, when we reflect that to ponder or consider is also figuratively known as 'weighing' in English (see **Demi-pension**).

**Persiflage** – light, playful or teasing talk. From *per* and *siffler*, to whistle.

**Pétard** – a farting anti-personnel device. A *pétard*, frequently and wrongly assumed to be a gallows thanks to Shakespeare's 'tis the sport to have the engineer hoist by his own petard', is a bomb or mine, and its name is derived from the French *péter*, to fart, tilt or crepitate. Also to crackle. For those running short of words for botty-burps, the French word is derived from the Latin *pedere* and is related to the Greek *bdein* and, so we are told, the Lithuanian *bezdeti*, all of which denote the breaking of wind.

**Pétillant** – sparkling, of wine. A diminutive of *péter* (from Latin *pedere*) to fart, whence comes the expression, '*péter plus haut que son cul*' – to fart higher than one's rectum, which means to overestimate one's worth or to have a high opinion of oneself.

**Petite** – literally 'small' and, of course, feminine, and, hitherto, used of women and girls who do not correspond to any of the meanings of the word 'big'

– fat, porcine, grotesquely gross, revoltingly corpulent, burly, brawny, statuesque etc. We may even hear it used of quite tall women as a qualification – 'Yes, she's five foot ten and fit, but she's actually quite petite,' but it has generally been used of women as short as they are slight. Of late, however, marketing men, attempting to flatter those who resemble uncooked cottage-loaves or semi-deflated barrage-balloons, have taken to appending this word to improbable dress-sizes, so that we find '42 *petite*' and other such gibberish which renders the term all but meaningless.

**Petite amie** – 'little friend'. Otherwise girlfriend, female lover.

**Petit four** – 'three and a bit,' says Pumphrey. He is wearing the kilt tonight. A *petit four* is a little cake or other *pâtisserie* confection, habitually served at dessert or to the ladies with coffee. The words mean 'little oven', which is a trifle strange.

**Petit maître** – literally 'little master'. A term with disparate meanings. Artisans such as cabinet-makers, jewellers, engravers and clockmakers, generally working alone or with apprentices of their own kith and kin rather than having large *ateliers* were frequently so described either by merit of the perceived minor nature of their crafts *vis-à-vis* the great arts or of their status *vis-à-vis* the great houses – the solitary dressmaker in relation to Worth or the Spitalfields cabinet-maker to Waring and Gillow. Equally, certain artists have been thus damned with faint praise in that they unquestionably dwell on the slopes of Olympus but are not deemed to belong in the halls of Parnassus at the summit. To confound the issue further, the term is also used to designate a fop.

**Pièce de résistance/d'occasion** – the (never 'a') *pièce de résistance* is the principal or outstanding work of an entire canon or career or of a particular exhibition, group of work, period etc. or the main or fanciest course of a meal. The *résistance* here is to the erosion of time, fashion and memory, so, it is estimated, the 'enduring piece'. A *pièce d'occasion* is the sort of thing that Laureates are paid to compose – a poem, piece of music or whatever, conceived and created for a specific event.

**Pied à terre** – literally 'foot to earth' – a stepping stone. In fact a small house or flat in town whose purpose is to supply a regular crib in which the occasional visitor can sleep and/or entertain.

**Pince-nez** – from *pincer*, to pinch (as in our own pincers), and *nez*, nose. A pair of eyeglasses held in place by a bridge athwart the nose's rather than by the user's hand (as with a *lorgnette* (*qv*)), the eye-socket (a monocle) or hooks about the user's ears (conventional spectacles).

**Piquant, pique, piqué** – all of these spring from the same French word – *piquer*, to prick, which in turn comes from an unknown Celtic source and supplies us with 'pike' in all its various pointy meanings, including that of the fish. *Piquant* today means 'pleasantly and stimulatingly sharp or pungent in flavour' and so, by extension, similarly stimulating or 'spicy' to the mind, though its sense was originally 'pricking', 'stinging' or 'bitter'.

*Pique* retains somewhat more the sense of 'nettling' or 'irritating' in the common phrase 'a fit of pique' or usages such as 'I was profoundly piqued not to receive an invitation'. The somewhat aberrant but not uncommon 'my curiosity was piqued' reverts to one of the word's original meanings ('pricked', 'stung into life'), though I suspect accidentally. In general, the French pronunciation makes the use of the verb uncommon. It is at once unneccessary, ambiguous and infelicitous. As a noun, however, it remains useful for a gradation of anger and resentment less persistent than irritation and less grave than rancour. *Piqué* is a woven fabric pattern of proud stitching, often of gold or other metallic thread.

**Pis aller** – Pumphrey is engaged in cursing a *sauce hollandaise*, which is far more important, and anyhow, I have no intention even of permitting him to see this entry. He is certain to inform me that he once lived in a sidestreet called Pis Aller, and, still worse, to believe it. In fact, the phrase means 'in the last resort' or (loathsome phrase) 'the worst scenario'.

**Placement** – the delicate art of placing guests at table according to gender, rank, predisposition, intellectual acumen, current or former intimacy and inappropriateness of sexual contact.

**Planchette** – 'little plank', a board on castors which mysteriously rolls in the direction in which it is pushed by people's fingers, causing the same people to ejaculate, 'Ooh! I'm not pushing, honest!' and 'M! My grandmother's auntie's name was Marigold!' and things like that, which they can subsequently blame on the dead, who probably don't mind.

**Plat du jour** – 'dish of the day'. Usually yesterday.

**Plié (or demi-plié)** – a ballet movement comprising a straight-backed squat with the feet turned outward. My plié was the talk of the Home Counties when I was four years old and attending Madame Vacani's Dance Academy at the Assembly Rooms in Alton. Alas for Terpsichore, I elected to lay down my tights and pluck up my pen. Literally folded or bent, from *plier*, whence too pliant, pliable and ply, meaning fold or layer.

**Plus ça change** ... – 'the more it changes ...', another expression with a shrug inalienably attached to it. A shortened version of the resigned dictum, '*Plus ça change, plus c'est la meme chose*', which is to say, 'the more circumstances change, the more history repeats itself'.

**Poilu** – 'an hairy man', from the Latin *pilus*, a hair. Originally an epithet applied to French soldiers returning from the front during the Great War of 1914–1918, and supposedly a tribute to their superabundant virility no less than their dishevelled and unkempt state. In gay and heterosexual slang, but particularly in the gay variety, in that value is still placed there upon dead rat moustaches and abundant body hair – a stud, a hunk.

**Pointillisme** – from *pointiller* – to speckle or mark with dots. A technique of painting favoured by certain Impressionists and Post-Impressionists, notably Georges Seurat, whereby the effects of light are rendered by the application of tiny dots of pure colour rather than by the mixing of pigments.

**Politesse** – politeness, good manners. Really there is nothing much to say about this rather prim borrowing, which is generally used in the faintly silly phrase *toujours la politesse* – always politeness. Admittedly 'politeness' does not trip lightly off the tongue. The only interesting thing about both the English and the French forms is that they are derived from the same origin as 'polish' – the Latin *polire*, to smooth or buff. It was not until eighteenth century that the sense of 'well-mannered' was assumed into this past participle.

**Pomade** – any highly scented oil or spirit for application to the hair and scalp, originally from the Italian *pomata*, in turn from *poma*, an apple, which implies that the scent of the original, the ur-pomade, was that of apples.

**Pommes sautées, pommes frites etc.** – Pumphrey tells me that the *hollandaise* has liaised (*qv*), that the asparagus water is walloping nicely and that the fish is all ready to be 'whanged' in the oven. He also, glancing over my shoulder, informs me that the terms *pommes sautées* and *pommes frites* originate among French emigrants to Australia, and denote various things which such people like to do to unsuspecting English people. So, according to him, a *pomme sautée* is an Englishwoman (or man if he runs into a ballet dancer, he says) 'jumped', and a *pomme frite* such an Englishman or woman when bending to pick up a coin in Kununurra or, as it might be, Wagga Wagga. As the common people say, 'What is he like?' In fact, these are potatoes (*pommes de terre*) *sautées* or fried, which are, in fact, precisely the same thing.

**Pompadour** – a sort of giant quiff of hair, swept back from the brow and arising in a rampant wave, much favoured by males in the 1950s. Females used to do the same thing, and even had a special pad or roll of paper over which they would construct such an edifice in order to afford it height. Named after Jean Toni Fish (Jeanne Antoinette Poisson), Marquise de Pompadour (1721–64), Louis XV's mistress, who is generally seen in her portraits sporting such a style.

**Portmanteau** – literally 'carry cloak (or garment)', and indeed a *portmanteau* was a splendid leather case divided into two equal sections in which one might convey large frocks or suits of clothing and the accessories and appurtenances thereto. It was surely the compendious nature of this luggage which gave rise to the figurative sense of combining two or more distinct things in one, as in a '*portmanteau* word', which is a mongrel bred of two or more others.

**Pose plastique** – 'plastic', of course, means 'readily moulded or formed', whence 'plastic surgery' (surgery intended to shape or reshape), 'plastic explosive' and the generic term for petroleum derivative resins. A *pose plastique* is a *tableau vivant* (*qv*) consisting of a collection of attitudes struck by people (usually, thank heaven, pretty, naked women), for the delectation of theatrical audiences. The Windmill Theatre in London became famous for never closing during the Blitz and for its *poses plastiques*.

**Poseur** – an admirable adolescent or an absurd adult so self-conscious and self-important that he or she attitudinises or postures and adopts views calculated – or, at least, intended – to impress. **Poseuse** exists but is far rarer.

**Poste restante** – 'mail remaining' – an address to which post can be sent to await the intended recipient; the department of a post office providing this service.

**Potager** – a kitchen garden. Also, sometimes, for no clear reason, *potagère*. The word actually means one who, or, rather, that which, makes *potages* or thick soups.

**Pot-au-feu** – we have our 'hotpots' and the French their *pots-au-feu*, or 'pots on the fire'. So long as we do not get involved in the totally absurd academic discussions as to what are or should be the ingredients of traditional peasant foods (many idiots will contend that the Cornish pasty must contain this or can in no circumstances contain that, whereas a Cornish *bonne femme*, untroubled by such gibbering, would surely have counted cat among the *bona fide* ingredients had one been passing), these are all but identical, being slow-cooked stews of cheap gelatinous cuts of meat, vegetables and grain or potatoes.

**Pot-pourri** – 'rotten pot', a translation of the Spanish dish, *olla podrida*, and once applied in French too to a stew, but today used of mixed dried flower-petals, seed-heads and spices, intended to suffuse the air with its scents.

**Pouf/pouffe** – the sea-trout has been whanged, and I have no intention of distracting Pumphrey by asking him for his definition of this word, thank you. It denotes a cushion, generally of leather or plush, with a flat, stable base, intended for use as a seat or footrest in rooms called 'lounges' or 'front rooms'. The origins of the word are onomatopoeic.

**Poule, poule au pot, poulet, poule de luxe** – a *poule* is a hen, but the word is widely used to mean a young woman, usually with slightly rounder heels than her prim sisters. A *poule de luxe* is such a charming creature who has turned her hobby to profitable use. She is a high-class prostitute (and anyone who believes these words to be oxymoronic is … oh, well, never mind). A *poule au pot* is a slowly stewed hen and a *poulet* a chicken.

**Pourboire** – 'for a drink' – a tip or gratuity.

**Pour encourager les autres** – 'to encourage others'. A dry witticism from Voltaire in response to the unjust execution of the scrupulous, honest and gallant Admiral John Byng for failing to relieve Minorca from French siege in 1756. In England, Voltaire wrote just three years later, '*il est bon de tuer de temps en temps un amiral pour encourager les autres*', it is considered good to kill an admiral from time to time to encourage the others. This reflects the widespread international outrage at the Admiralty's high-handed, self-exculpatory victimisation of a fine officer.

**Pourparler** – an informal discussion in preparation for formal conference or debate.

**Précis** – a lost art form; a summary, usually literary but sometimes oral, from the French for concise, succinct, condensed or even 'precise'.

**Prêt à porter** – of clothes, ready to wear, off-the-peg.

**Princesse lointaine** – a distant princess. An unattainable, idealised female object of desire or aspirational, purportedly romantic love, a Beatrice, a silly role which has afforded some few of its performers material advantage while denying the huge majority of their sisters self-esteem and good sex.

**Profiterole** – a small ball of *choux* pastry (*qv*) generally filled with cream or occasionally with a savoury *farce* (*qv*). Originally in English a small item of food, superfluous to that served at the principal tables, intended to be a 'little profit' or perk for the staff.

**Protégé/e** – one enjoying the care, sponsorship and often tutelage of a patron, usually senior in age or position. From *protéger*, to protect.

**Puissance** – literally power or might. Now the name of a show-jumping event in which butazolidin-stuffed horses trained for some reason to perform like circus fleas attempt to jump as high as possible vertically.

***Quand même*** – none the less, all the same.

***Quartier*** – a district of a city. Save in the case of the *quartier Latin*, which enjoys mythical status, Parisian *quartiers* are invariably referred to only by their ordinal numbers – *seizième*, *huitième* and the like.

***Quel*** ... – decidedly camp English usage meaning 'What a ...', as in '*Quel surprise!*' or even, macaronically, '*Quel bum!*'

***Quenelle*** – an ellipsoidal member of the noble family of dumplings, which includes *gnocchi*, *dim sum* etc., a *quenelle* is generally made with fish (most commonly pike) flesh and poached in *court bouillon*. The origin of the term is unknown.

**Qui vive** – the French want their heroes and leaders to live, and express this desire whenever possible in order to demonstrate their loyalties, clamouring (albeit circumspectly) '*Vive le Roi!*' '*Vive la République!*' or '*Vive le vainqueur!*' (which saves time) at every possible opportunity. A sentry, then, anxious to establish the affiliations of an approaching stranger, would challenge not with 'Who goes there?' but with '*Qui vive?*' or 'Long live who?' to which the interloper would respond, 'Vive someone or other.' Whether '*Vive* no one in particular' established you as a harmless neutral or Swiss, I cannot discover. To be 'on the *qui vive*,' therefore, is to be on the alert, on guard.

***Raison(s) d'état*** – reason(s) of state. Politicians believe that their thoughts should be public and their parts private. When others deem their tawdry parts mildly more interesting than their workaday thoughts, they get very aggravated. It is then that they grab the sponge of 'national security', 'the public interest' or, if even these words sound too brutally harsh, '*raisons d'état*'.

***Raison d'être*** – reason for existence. The essential purpose of a person, thing or event. The assumption that a person can have such a teleological 'reason', as distinct from the mechanistic ('because my parents got drunk and had sex') is characteristically fanciful and self-justifying.

**Raisonné** – see **Catalogue raisonné**.

**Rapport** – from *rapporter*, to bring or carry back. So a relationship of mutuality, of shared trust and understanding, an affinity between people and places or animals.

**Rapportage** – is reporting, pure and simple, as distinct from the more imaginative, discursive or creative forms of journalism or narration. So committees, debating chambers and the like have **rapporteurs**, whose function it is essentially to keep minutes and to relay them to the public, shareholders or other higher authorities.

**Rapprochement** – 'reapproaching'. The restoration of *entente* (*qv*) after *détente* (*qv*), a re-establishment of amicable or, at least, businesslike relations between states or persons.

**Ravissant/e** – 'ravishing', from *ravir*, originally to seize, take away, plunder or, at least in the sense of the Sabine women, to rape. The word indeed comes from the Latin *rapere*, which had the sense of seizing or abduction, whence too came 'ravenous' of wild animals (but not 'raven', which is a proper old word) and so the modern sense of that which agreeably transports us willy-nilly (as it were).

**Réchauffé/e** – reheated, warmed up, from the French *échauffer*, to warm. So what, I hear you ask, has a *chauffeur* to do with warming (aside from the inevitable rumours, of course, which I have known on occasion to be true)? Well, the *chauffeur* was originally the stoker of the engine – that is, the man who kept it fuelled and heated in order to generate power. *Réchauffé* is another euphemism supposedly to disguise the fact that we are talking about reheated leftovers.

**Recherché/e** – well, *rechercher* is to seek out, so *recherché* means rare, obscure, elusive, eclectic – that which must be assiduously sought out.

**Reculer pour mieux sauter** – how on earth does that startlingly original mind come up with some of its ideas? 'To sit down (or have a rectal transplant?) in order to fry cats?' is Pumphrey's suggestion to explain this phrase. I have never even heard of a rectal transplant, nor of people frying cats, though Pumphrey assures me that he has experience of both in his travels. He is a most remarkable person. Alas, this expression has nothing to do with frying or, indeed, recta or cats. It means 'to withdraw (or recoil) the better to jump'. When I explained this to Pumphrey, he told me that he has experience of this too. I do not disbelieve him. The image, of course, is that of an animal recoiling in order to spring, but the expression is more commonly used of a tactical retreat or withdrawal with the intention, rarely fulfilled, of returning restored to the fray.

**Régime** – curious word, in that it is derived from the Latin *regimen*, meaning 'rule' or 'government', which word we borrowed direct and have retained with precisely the same meanings as the French word. So 'régime' and 'regimen' in English are interchangeable as meaning healthy lifestyle or course of diet, exercise, prayer, meditation etc., which appears to have been the original meaning of both borrowings. Subsequently, both words have also been used to denote their original Latin meaning – government or administration.

**Règlement** – the French refer to flagellation as *le vice anglais* (*qv*), though Sade, of course, the cult's high-priest and prophet, was a Frenchman. *Règlement* or regulation, and the amassing of *règlements* or regulations governing every aspect of human existence are unquestionably *le vice francais*, and, indeed, *belgique*. Little black dresses and the Moulin Rouge today leave the Frenchman unmoved, while little black books and red tape cause him to squirm and suppurate in a most unseemly manner.

**Réligieuse** – a nun or an iced cream cake, depending. Appearance is a good guide.

**Remuage** – the periodic turning of a bottle of wine, particularly champagne, to shift sediment. A **remueur** is someone who does this.

**Rendezvous** – an appointment to meet at a specific place. *Rendez-vous* simply means 'present yourself or yourselves', so it is as if the request RSVP (*qv*) had been rendered as a noun phrase – 'must dash. I've got an RSVP at the Palace' – a usage thank God unknown. It is curious that so formal an injunction should have come to be used, as often as not, to denote an informal and private prearranged meeting. The term entered English no later than the sixteenth century, when it was commonly written 'rendevous'. The need to 'correct' this by adding the French 'z', so making it a 'multi-cultural society', immigrant word, rather than an integrated British one, occurred to no one until the eighteenth century.

**Repartee** – this, which means witty replies, is not, strictly a French word at all, but is modelled on *reparti(e)*, an altogether more possible past participle, from *repartir*, to set out again. The derivation is probably best understood if we consider the similar word 'sortie', a sally or setting out. This word is used in English not only in a military sense but with reference to conversation. If we have a conversational sortie or, as a chess-player would say, gambit, it is plausible that our opponent should respond with a *repartie*.

**Repertoire/répertoire** – why, oh, why? We had 'repertory' (borrowed direct from the Latin *repertorium* – inventory or list) before Shakespeare, but some pretentious mid-nineteenth-century musical or theatrical person (probably a critic) felt the urgent need to render it in the French form instead.

**Reprise** – a resumption or repetition of an action, an encore, from the past participle of *reprendre*, to take back or take again. The word has been used in English to mean an amount deducted for expenses, a sum due to tenants from landlords and compensation. In the seventeenth century, it came to mean the resumption of something arrested, in the nineteenth, the reversal of a melody to an initial theme.

**Restaurant/restaurateur** – the language has its intrinsic lessons which can profitably be heeded. Politicians, for example, should be reminded daily that the word 'minister' means 'servant'. So too a large number of *restaurateurs* might profitably recall that their function is *restaurer*, to restore, and that their establishments boldly and generally inaccurately declare this to be their purpose. Until well into the eighteenth century, eating houses were specialist, and each regulated by their own guilds or trading associations – the *rôtisseurs* roasted, the *pâtissiers* made pastries and pies, the *aubergistes* could offer wine but not food, the *traiteurs* made prepared dishes such as stews and so on. Then *restaurant* meant a thin soup, intended to restore, and a *restaurateur* was

PAR AVION

one who made such broths or stocks. In time, the *restaurant* appropriated the right to prepare a wide variety of foods, and, in 1786, the first *restaurant*, more or less as we know it, but still no doubt restorative, was registered. Then the French Revolution swept away the guilds and their restrictions, and more catholic eating houses open to the general public spread fast.

**Résumé** – one of the most boring entries in this book, a *résumé* is, of course, a summary or précis (*qv*), particularly of a person's life or career, whence the Americans derive the sense of a *curriculum vitae*.

**Retroussé/e** – 'turned up'. Always used of noses, but seldom of, say, nipples or penises, in both of which it were – and is – a far more generally desirable quality. By derivation, the word sinply means 'twisted back', from the French *trusser*, which comes in turn from the Latin *torquere*, to twist. It describes an infantile trait once highly valued in girls (no Wodehouse or musical comedy heroine, for example, ever had a straight or Roman nose) but today less generally coveted.

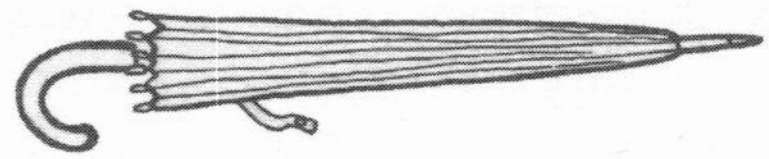

**Réveille** – 'someday I'm going to murder the bugler… and then I'll get that other pup, the one who wakes the bugler up, and spend the rest of my life in bed …' Irving Berlin's song of hate for the military *réveille* or wake-up call found an echo in hundreds of thousands of soldiers. *Réveillez*, from which the word comes, is simply the French command, 'wake up', but it has a militaristic origin, in that *veiller* is derived from the Latin *vigilare*, to keep watch or to be alert, so a *réveille* (often pronounced in English revelly or revally) is an injunction to resume watch.

**Revenant** – from *revenir*, to come back, whence one returned from the dead, though strictly anyone returned, such as the prodigal, might so be termed.

**Rêverie** – one of a whole series of diverse words taken from *rêver*, to be delirious, which include *rêver*, to dream, 'rave' and 'revelry'. The connotations of delirium and wild frolicking contained in these English words belonged to *rêverie* as well until the seventeenth century, when associations of 'dreaminess' – the delightful wanderings of daydream – came to dominate. Today, *rêverie* is almost interchangeable with 'daydream', and quite as pretty.

**Revue** – a comical, generally satirical selection of songs and sketches, generally with one uniting theme. From the French word for a survey.

**Richesse** – see **Embarras de** …

**Ricochet** – absolutely nothing to do with Irishmen, but in truth, nobody knows whence this word for the rebound of a missile or projectile comes, save in that there was a mediaeval tradition of the *fable du ricochet*, a tale in which the teller consistently evaded or threw back all questions.

**Rien ne va plus** – 'nothing more goes', or 'no more bets' – the *croupier's* (*qv*) call when once the *roulette* (*qv*) wheel is set spinning.

**Riposte** – a fencing term, meaning a prompt thrust in response to another. Interestingly, this comes from the Latin *respondere*, to reply, but *riposte* recovered this conversational sense only when it had been sharpened by fencing usage in the 1850s. It now means a quick and usually witty or damaging verbal retort.

**Risqué** – naughty but not (or not necessarily in the case of a *double entendre* (*qv*)) indecent. Evidently from *risquer*, to risk.

**Rodomontade** – sometimes inexplicably rendered 'rhodomontade', as if the word had something to do with roses, as with 'rhododendron'. In fact, a *rodomontade* is a boast or brag or boastful speech or puffed-up and braggartly behaviour or habits. It comes from the character Rodomonte, the braggart pagan king in Ariosto's *Orlando Furioso* (1532).

**Roman** – a novel, whence **roman à clef** (novel with a key, which is to say a novel in which characters and events are closely based on real equivalents), **roman à thèse** (novel with a thesis, so a boring, unrealistic didactic novel propounding or illustrating a concept), **roman fleuve** (river novel, or a saga of several generations of the same family or community) and **roman policier** (detective novel).

**Roué** – a rake or dissipated man. Literally 'wheeled' or, more specifically, 'broken on the wheel', the fate thought suitable by the puritanical and censorious for the debauched friends of the French Regent, the Duc d'Orléans.

**Rouge** – red colouring for cheeks (blusher) or, less commonly, lips. Also a verb, meaning to apply such colour. The origin, from modern French *rouge* (red), in turn from the Latin *rubeus*, were obvious to a British babe in arms, and the word, simply meaning 'bright red' has been part of the language since the Norman invasion. We retain Middle English titles such as Rouge Croix (though the heraldic term for 'red' is 'gules'), but the term seems to have sunk into desuetude until reborrowed with its modern, specific meaning in eighteenth century.

**Roulette** – gambling game, literally 'little wheel'.

**Routier** – a long-distance lorry-driver, which term became the name of a guide to cafés, roadhouses and restaurants recommended for such people.

**RSVP** – *Répondez s'il vous plaît*, commonly embossed (but far more agreeably engraved) at the feet of invitation cards. Why? Who knows? Another desperate attempt to acquire refinement by the assumption of French, and, perhaps, to avoid associations with Daisy des Is on her tandem …

**Sabotage/saboteur** – deliberate damage inflicted on property to impair the activities of an enemy. The word comes from the French *sabot*, which is a carved wooden shoe or clog worn by peasants. It has been suggested that the later word is derived from the practice of striking workers of throwing their *sabots* into the works in order to break the machines and suspend production. This is a charming conceit, but appears to be untrue. The verb *saboter* also means to blunder, to execute clumsily or cack-handedly, from association either with the coarse carving of the shoes or with the clattering footfalls of their wearers, so the word seems to allude to the damage which may be done by clumsy peasant workers.

**Sabreur** – one who wields a sabre, so generally a cavalry officer, though the term is almost invariably used in English in the phrase *beau sabreur*, referring to a gallant, or, as the English would once have said, 'a gay blade', and the weapon referred to is seldom actually a sabre.

**Salle privée** – a private room in a casino where high rollers may disport and win or lose serious sums of money. Private and *privé* are both derived from *privare*, which wisely has the senses at once of 'to deprive' and 'to liberate'. The philosopher Kristofferson tells us that 'Freedom's just a word for nothing left to lose'. This message is contained in the meanings of 'privacy' and 'private', where privation (of public office and fame) is synonymous with the luxuries of solitude and freedom.

**Salon (des refusés etc.)** – how agreeable to find a French word whose origin is Teutonic rather than Latin. *Salon*, today meaning a reception room or large hall, does come from the Italian *salone*, which has the same meaning, but this is derived from the Old High

German *sal*, a great hall or house, whence also comes *salle* as in *salle à manger* (dining room), *salle de bains* (bathroom) etc. In the late nineteenth century, people started to hold *salons*, or gatherings of the talented or fashionable. This word was transferred by association to the Parisian equivalent of the British Royal Academy Summer Exhibition, an annual exhibition of paintings and sculptures. In 1863, Napoleon III ordered the foundation of a *salon des refusés*, where rejected works were exhibited, and the Impressionists made a virtue of their regular presence there.

**Sang froid** – 'cold blood'. Coolness under fire or amid passions and pressure. A French name for a British product, Pumphrey says.

**Sans** – without, as in Jacques' man in 'second childishness and mere oblivion, sans teeth, sans eyes, sans taste, sans everything', in *As You Like It*. **Sans serif**, therefore, is any one of many typefaces without serif (cross-stroke or tail) while **sans culottes** (without breeches) were the scruffy, radical, impoverished and impassioned cannon-fodder of the French Revolution. A **sans pareil** is one without peer, and **sans reproche** means blameless, wholly exonerated and exempt from reproach.

**Sans peur et sans reproche** – fearless and blameless. A magnificent tribute originally applied to Pierre du Terrail, Chevalier de Bayard (1477–1524), who scored some sensational victories for Louis XII and Francis I before dying in action defending the pass of the River Sesia in Italy. The phrase is now more widely used to mean 'with total licence', so, for example, 'Further up the beach, however, visitors may divest themselves of all clothing *sans peur et sans reproche* …'.

**Sauter/sauté/e** – *sauter* is to leap or to jump, from *saltare*, to leap or dance, but in English *sauté/sautée* as an adjective means fried quickly and with little fat or, as a noun, food cooked thus. This sense is almost certainly due to the tossing of foods in the pan during this process in order to ensure the rapid transfer of heat to all surfaces without allowing any one to remain on the base for long enough to burn, rather than to the spontaneous responses of many foods to such cooking. *Sauter* as a transitive verb is therefore strictly incorrect, while 'to *sauter*' is simply an abomination. '*Sautéed*' is also widely used, and downright silly.

**Sauve qui peut** – 'save whoever can', a panicked rout, a stampede.

**Savant** – a sage, an authority, but see **idiot savant**.

**Savoir faire** – literally 'to know how to do', the natural grace and sensitivity which enables its possessor to act with tact and courtesy in unforeseen circumstances.

**Savoir vivre** – as above, 'to know how to live', or, here, to know how to live well – to attain, that is, that felicitous balance between sybaritism and asceticism, hard work and leisure which makes for serenity.

**Séance** – a sitting or, as we would say, session, which might be of a learned society, a committee or whatever. It shares an origin as well as a meaning with our 'session,' since *séance*, which comes from the Old French *seoir*, to sit (now *asseoir*) is derived from the Latin *sedere*. The spiritualistic séance, at which the credulous gather to conjure spirits from the vasty deep, is first recorded, unsurprisingly, in the mid-nineteenth century.

**Seigneur** – see **Grand seigneur** and **Droit de seigneur**.

**Silhouette** – a monochrome outline portrait, usually in black on a paler field, named after one Étienne de Silhouette, the French Minister of Finance in 1759. The problem is that we do not know how or why his name came to be given to this technique. Some have surmised that the coining had satirical intent: this, it was implied, was the only sort of portrait that anyone would be able to afford once old Étienne had finished imposing absurd constraints on just about everything in order to finance the Seven Years' War. Apparently he himself made very poor outline portraits which he hung at his Bry-sur-Marne *château*. Or was this a reference to the brevity of his tenure (a mere seven months), which might have meant that a lot of portraits and official likenesses were left incomplete, with the robes of office all painted and the head and shoulders left blank, awaiting a sitting that never took place? I tend to favour this last explanation, though I would be happier with it were anyone to demonstrate that there were documents or medals, say, or any articles in wide currency, which might have borne M. de Silhouette's portrait in profile …

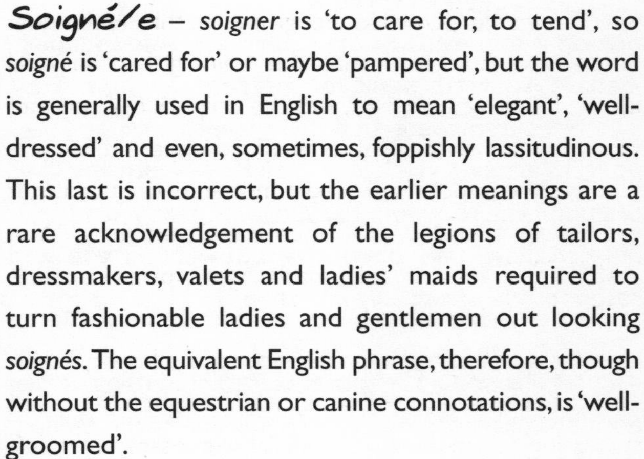

**Sobriquet (also soubriquet)** – nickname. Originally in French a chuck under the chin. Origin unknown.

**Soi-disant** – self-styled, pretending or purporting to be …

**Soigné/e** – *soigner* is 'to care for, to tend', so *soigné* is 'cared for' or maybe 'pampered', but the word is generally used in English to mean 'elegant', 'well-dressed' and even, sometimes, foppishly lassitudinous. This last is incorrect, but the earlier meanings are a rare acknowledgement of the legions of tailors, dressmakers, valets and ladies' maids required to turn fashionable ladies and gentlemen out looking *soignés*. The equivalent English phrase, therefore, though without the equestrian or canine connotations, is 'well-groomed'.

**Soirée** – Pumphrey has written, 'What you say when you've been noightée', which is surprisingly amusing, but of course, a *soirée* is an entertainment or 'at home' held in the evening, from the French word meaning 'all of the evening' (so *jour*, day, and *an*, year, become *journée* and *année* when we wish to convey the sense of the whole day or year). Today, the term is generally restricted to musical evenings (*soirées musicales*).

**Sois sage** – oh, so euphonious an injunction to behave. *Sois sage* – literally 'be wise', may be an affectionate 'take care', as spoken to a young person setting out on a gap-year, say, or a stern but soft-sounding, 'Behave yourself, punk, or prepare to have your intestines removed, tied in sheepshanks and fed upon by passing pigs.' Very useful, save with the likes of Pumphrey, to whom I said it very gently last night, only to have him open one cobwebbed eye and respond, 'Major, actually, old chap.'

**Soixante-neuf** – this is quite an amusing sexual position enabling mutual oral stimulation of the genitals, in which, if the heads are taken to represent the circular sections of the numerical figures, the couple so engaged form a shape not dissimilar to that formed by the number '69', though, of course, the circular section of the '6' should be raised somewhat and that of the '9' lowered, and the two digits must be placed very adjacent …

**Solitaire** – 'solitary', whence the name of any number of card games played by one player only. The original sense of the word in English was of a recluse or a widow, then of a solitary jewel, usually a diamond, but the games which I always thought of as 'Patience', believing *solitaire* to be an American introduction, were in fact so known in England in the mid-eighteenth century. The game in which marbles jump one another until only one is left (is it the solitary marble or the solitary player which suggested the name?) was so named soon afterwards, and it was perhaps the popularity of this game which occasioned the introduction of 'Patience' as a distinct one-person game.

**Sommelier** – the wine-steward or wine-waiter in a restaurant. I am ambivalent about these. On the one hand, there are true *sommeliers*, who are enthusiastic, hugely knowledgeable and, like most people with a passion for their subject, eager to impart that knowledge. On the other, there are those who sneer at us who order house-wine (well, who selected it as house-wine?) or water and believe themselves – who have been paid to drink fine wines – to be superior to those who must pay for them. Of the former, it should be remembered that the true Master Sommelier (the Court is English, so *maître sommelier* is pretentious nonsense) has passed three exacting examinations in Theory, Tasting and Practical Service. With the latter, it is good to remember, and to remind them, that the word *sommelier* is thought to be derived from *sauma*, the Latin for 'pack-saddle', because wine used to be driven to market in mule-trains, and the muleteer who drove this transport and sold the casks was the *sommelier*. A chorus of 'The Donkey Serenade' does not come amiss.

**Son et lumière** – 'sound and light', which just about says it all. A nocturnal entertainment, usually *en plein air* and usually in Britain rained off, featuring sound and light effects along with music, drama and the like.

**Sorbet/sorbetière** – *sorbet* is the French version of 'sherbet'. Sherbet, meaning cooling drink of fruit juice and syrup, comes from the Arabic *sharbah*, *sharbat*, a drink, and was introduced into English as 'zerbet' in the late sixteenth century. Only in 1891 do we find the word used of a fruit or flower-flavoured ice. Why, then, have we adopted the

French word, which is nowhere near as pleasant or mellifluous? Partly gastronomic snobbery, partly because the word 'sherbet' was adopted by confectioners in the mid-nineteenth century to denote a flavoured powder which could be eaten undilute, particularly when sucked up from a 'sherbet fountain', or mixed with water to created an effervescent sweet drink (hands up those who remember Cremola Foam?). This was all too frighteningly *infra dig* for our European gastrognomes, whose water-ices became *sorbets* instead. A *sorbetière* is a domestic mechanical churn in which ice-creams or *sorbets* gyrate as they are frozen.

**Soubrette** – a stock character in French drama and light opera, particularly of the comic variety, the *soubrette* is a pert, playful, seductive maidservant who, if she were a cartoon character, would have a large arrow pointing at her beneath a bubble stating '*OH LÀ LÀ*!!' Usually briefly clad (since the late nineteenth century at least) in a fetching little cap, a black dress, a frilly white apron and black stockings, she is at once invariably good for a tumble and for intimate details of her mistress and her household in furtherance of the plot.

**Soupçon** – 'suspicion', generally used of taste, in which a *soupçon* of a certain flavouring or ingredient may be a 'hint' or 'slight suggestion of', or a smidgin, a pinch, a tiny quantity.

**Souvenir** – from French *se souvenir*, to remember, which comes from *subvenire* come to mind or come up (from below). The word was originally borrowed to convey the sense of 'a memory' for which we already had a perfectly adequate word, so it came to mean a token of remembrance or a memento instead, usually at first of a person (locks of hair and the like) but increasingly of royal funerals, battles, sexual encounters, visits to Corby and the other events so memorable in theory but forgettable in reality that they require enduring prompts.

**Specialité (de la maison etc.)** – well, speciality, from the Latin *specialis* meaning 'particular', 'one of a kind' which came in turn from *species*, sort or kind. To be honest, this word never seems to have been borrowed wholesale in its French form, save in the days before English spelling was standardised when *specialité* was merely an alternative spelling. Only when restaurants pretending to sophistication started branding particular dishes *specialité de la maison* do we find the word cropping up in self-consciously Gallic form. Nowadays, pubs tend to call them 'specials' which is far more comfortable.

**Succès d'estime/de scandale/fou** – a success (*or succès*) is, stricly, an outcome, a consequence of causation merely, but it came to mean the accomplishment of something aspired to somewhere about the sixteenth century. The more general sense of – well, what? Wealth? Good Fortune? Health? – is a typical nineteenth-century concept, and totally meaningless. The borrowed French phrases are more specific. A *succès d'estime* is a success of opinion – a critical success, that is, generally as distinct from a commercial; a *succès fou* is a mad success, or one which causes widespread cheers and the flinging of undergarments; while a *succès de scandale* is a success due to popular or press outrage, either at the work enjoying such success or at some antic of the authors.

**Suède** – reversed hide, and leather with a soft nappe. *Suède*, of course, means Sweden, and the word came to be used thus because such inside-out leather gloves (as distinct from the usual right-side-out dog or pony skin varieties) were introduced from, or in the style of, Sweden in the 1880s and became known as *gants de Suède* (gloves of, or from, Sweden). When the same material was used for shoes (graphically known as brothel-creepers in English) and other garments, the word too was transformed.

**Suite** – see **En suite**

**Sympathique, 'sympa'** – commonly and correctly cited as an example of a French word for which we have no equivalent, *sympathique* broadly means, of a person, 'pleasant, agreeable, easily related to or readily understood and appreciated'. The precise meaning eludes English because it relates to the user as much as the subject, and entails no inherent value judgements, so 'He is a total swine but very *sympathique*, is a perfectly acceptable sentiment. *Sympa* is an *argot (qv)* abbreviation which has crossed the Channel. Décor, houses, horses etc. may also be thus described.

**Tableau/tableau vivant** – a *tableau* is a picture, from, of course, *table*, which descends to French as to English from *tabula*, the Latin for board, slab or table. The use of 'board' in English to mean 'table' (usually found in 'bed and board' or the bowel-witheringly whimsical 'festive board') and the fact that most early paintings were on board and many carvings or inscriptions on slabs establishes the link. In English, the French word for a picture is generally used of a picture's subject or of people or things arrayed as for a picture, so most *tableaux* are in fact *tableaux vivants* in which people are arrested in action on stage or elsewhere as in *poses plastiques* (*qv*).

**Table d'hôte** – 'host's table'. I here refer you to the entry for *à la carte* wherein I mentioned that the traveller would once have dined on the same fare as that enjoyed by an innkeeper and his family, and, generally, at that same communal table. The *table d'hôte* remains, therefore, the set meal offered at an all-in price at an eating establishment.

**Tant mieux/tant pis** – so much the better, so much the worse. Nicolas Bentley, of course, rendered these two phrases non-alphabetically, giving the meaning of *tant pis, tant mieux* as 'auntie is feeling so much better since she visited the Ladies', or some such – a silliness worthy of Pumphrey himself. *Tant mieux* is generally used after a conditional clause – 'If you can make it by five o clock, *tant mieux*' – while *tant pis* is frequently used on its own in acceptance of bad, but not grave, tidings. 'Shit happens' is, I believe, the contemporary English – well, American – version. Expressive, if syntactically dubious.

**Tarot** – cards, generally now known in Britain only for the arcana, or arcane cards, with which fortunes are told, but in fact derived from playing cards still widely used for games such as *scopa* and *briscola* in

Latin countries, featuring suits of clubs, money, cups and swords (*spade* in Italian, whence our spades). These are known as the *Tarocci*, whence the French (who invented our later playing cards) derive *tarot*.

**Temps perdu** – time lost. '*Eheu fugaces, postume – postume*,' as my taxi driver frequently mutters (I think), quoting Horace as these chaps will when I bid him wait another few minutes on the double yellow line in front of the Queen's Head on St Uncumber Street. What he means, of course, was wittily summarised by Richard Barham in a following line, 'Years glide away, and are lost to me, lost to me!' This is the sense of *temps perdu*, a phrase taken, of course, from Proust's interminable memoir '*À la Recherche du Temps perdu*' ('In search of lost time'), which I can commend to anyone seeking to lose a great deal more.

**Terrasse** – originally a terrace as we use the word – that is a flat, raised surface on a mound of earth on which to walk or *flâner* (*qv*) – but today generally a paved area outside a restaurant or café where people may dine or drink.

**Tête à tête** – that disgraceful Pumphrey suggests that this has something to do with our Sapphic friends. I tell him that he has a one-track mind, but he says, 'Well, if you know how to drive, why not stick to the most atrractive track?' Of course a *tête à tête* is a 'head to head', but, whereas 'head to head' is used in English to convey the sense of a clash or *contretemps* (*qv*), *tête à tête* means a private, discreet but not necessarily intimate meeting or discussion between two people.

**Thé dansant** – 'dancing tea', a phrase conjuring a Disneyesque picture barely stranger than the thing which it in fact denotes. A *thé dansant* is an extraordinary entertainment or social event which enabled temperance enthusiasts and those unwilling to pay nightclub or *palais de danse* (*qv*) prices none the less to tread a measure. This improbable blend of foxtrots and muffins is still occasionally revived in Scarborough and other such delightful spots.

**Tic** – a twitch or involuntary muscular convulsion or spasm. In French, this was an equine disease, but the term came into English as *tic douloureux* – dolorous or painful tic.

**Tisane** – a herbal tea, but formerly a medicinal barley water or infusion made with barley, from *ptisana*, the Greek word for peeled or husked barley (*ptissein* is to peel).

**Ton** – sense of style, fashionableness. The Marshal of Luxembourg in the eighteenth century, remarked of the Bible, '*Quel effroyable ton! Ah, Madame, quel dommage que le Saint Esprit eût aussi peu de goût!*' or 'What a frightful sense of style. Ah, madame, what a shame that the Holy Spirit had so little taste!'

**Tontine** – a very sporting tax-advantageous bet or insurance policy, now back in fashion, named after a Neapolitan banker named Lorenzo Tonti (1630–1695) who established the first recorded such system in order to raise French government loans. All participants in a *Tontine* pledge or lodge sums of money or, indeed, whole estates to a fund, draw incomes from that fund and earnestly pray that the other subscribers will die as soon as possible, since that income rises with each death, and the sole survivor scoops the entire pool.

**Touché!** – a fencing term, indicating acknowledgement that an opponent's sword has made a hit, whence the caption of one of the twentieth century's most famous cartoons (the great James Thurber, after Carl Rose), in which one combatant's head is seen flying from his shoulders. So, in conversation or debate, a gracious acknowledgement of 'a hit, a palpable hit'.

**Toujours gai** – always gay, or, rather, cheerful – a phrase that has survived despite changing meanings thanks to Don Marquis's masterly *Archy and Mehitabel*, in which the cat Mehitabel, though generally morose, repeatedly describes herself thus.

**Tour de force** – a feat of strength, whence any outstanding accomplishment or work.

**Tout court** – 'all short', by which is meant 'in short' or 'put simply ...' Pumphrey is playing up again, largely, I think, due to the Laphroaig, and maintains that this phrase means 'a crepitation in the presence of the monarch, as released by the Earl of Oxford ...'

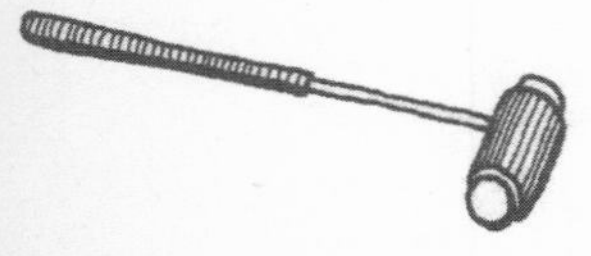

**Tout de suite** – ... and that this means 'a tilt on a sofa or a poppy wind on a *pouffe* (*qv*)'. I have absolutely no idea to what he refers. The phrase means, of course, in English as in French, 'at once'.

**Tout ensemble** – all together (as a command or injunction), or, as *le tout ensemble*, 'the whole kaboodle', all the component parts or people seen as a whole.

**Tout le monde** – 'all the world', so 'everyone' or 'everyone that matters', depending on the user of the phrase.

**Tracasserie** – *tracasser* is to vex oneself or to worry. *Tracasserie*, therefore, is a state of anxiety or vexation or, by association, a needless fuss.

**Tranche** – a slice (from Latin *truncare*). So one may be paid in *tranches* or instalments, or, rather horribly and gratuitously, anything performed or published in serial form may be described in terms of *tranches* of the whole. A singularly ugly and unnecessary usage.

**Triage** – sorting according to size, quality, urgency or importance. Most commonly used of medical care in crisis, and often mistakenly supposed to refer to sorting into three categories – trivial injuries, grave injuries and past help – and to be so derived, *triage* is in fact derived from the Old French *trier*, to pick or select, and refers to any 'prioritising' of limited resources. It is certainly a great deal prettier than that gross neologism …

**Tricoteuse** – knitting woman, from *tricoter*, to knit (which used to be called 'knotting' back then). The *tricoteuses* were women who sat knitting about the guillotine during the French Revolution. Their descendants are to be seen today at wrestling bouts and on television gameshows, less profitably employed but no less eager to see pain and indignity inflicted.

**Trompe l'oeil** – 'trick the eye'. A painting designed by the skilful use of light and shadow to cause an optical illusion of depth and so of reality.

**Trousseau** – we have the old word 'to truss', which means to bundle up, and the noun 'truss', which has thence come to mean a support, whether for a bridge or a belly. These, like *trousseau*, come from the Old French *trousse*, a bundle, *trousser*, to pack. A *trousseau* – a bride's clothing, linen etc., given to her before her nuptials – is therefore a small bundle – no doubt a stage further on from her 'bottom drawer' in which its components are stored.

**Tutoyer** – to address as *tu* and *toi* rather than *vous*, and so to address informally or intimately. Entirely wrongly, but not unamusingly, the parallel form *vousvoyer* has sprung up in contrast. The initiation of *tutoyant*, like kissing on one cheek rather than two or more, was once regarded as an exciting moment in the development of a relationship. Seriously posh Frenchmen still *vousvoient* their wives and dogs, but not their children or servants.

*Vaudeville* – a form of variety entertainment, featuring songs, sketches, speciality acts etc. Originally in English a light popular ditty, and thought to be derived from *Chanson de Vau de Vire*, song of the Valley of Vire. Vire in Normandy was the home of Olivier Basselin, a fifteenth-century poet, and it has been supposed that the transference from *vire* to *ville* was a popular error influenced by *ville*, town. If this seems a bit far-fetched, you are not alone in thinking it so. Other etymologists have suggested that the origins of *vau de vire* are dialectical, and come from *vauder*, to go, and *virer*, to turn.

**Vaut le voyage/le détour** – it's worth the journey/detour. Familiar clause from the Michelin restaurant guides which so describe worthy (and so, by definition, off-the-beaten-track) establishments. Often used in English to describe churches, pubs, men, women, or even, rather charmingly, books or ideas.

**Ventre à terre** – flat out, at full tilt. Literally 'belly to earth'. A glance at any eighteenth-century equestrian painting or engraving vividly illustrates how this expression came into being. Before the invention of photography demonstrated that a galloping horse is always in contact with the ground, it was thought that it proceeded in a series of flat bounds and, at high speeds, left the ground altogether and so proceeded *ventre à terre*.

**Vernissage** – 'varnishing', from the same source, the Latin *vernix*, a fragrant resin. Painters were permitted to touch up their work *in situ* on the eve of, or on a set day before, the opening of an exhibition. *Vernissage* therefore came to mean the event and the day on which it occurred, and today is often used of a Private View.

***Vers d'occasion*** – verse written for a special occasion.

***Vers libre*** – 'free verse', *soi-disant* poetry which pays no regard to prosody or rhyme. T.S. Eliot declared that there was no such thing. T.S. Eliot was right.

***Veuve*** – widow, but most commonly used as la Veuve, 'the widow', to refer to Veuve Clicquot champagne.

***Viande à pneus*** – 'meat for tyres', a most distasteful (but apposite in relation to Parisian drivers) French expression for pedestrians.

***Vice anglais, le*** – the 'English vice'. Many things, including tea-drinking, have been thus characterised, but the phrase is most commonly used of corporal punishment and thus of flagellation administered and received for pleasure.

***Vie en rose, la*** – 'life in pink', or, as we would say, 'life seen through rose-coloured spectacles'. The expression was popularised by Edith Piaf, who wrote the song of this name and, to a lesser extent, Marlene Dietrich, who delightfully droned it.

**Vieux jeu** – 'old game'. Old-fashioned, outdated.

**Vignette** – literally a little vine, whence a trailing, curling ornament in decorative work, a sort of graphic curlicue on a parchment or paper or a carved representation of foliage in architecture, whence again a small decorative sketch or ornamental montage or figure at the head or tail of a page. In the nineteenth century, the word came to mean a brief, anecdotal life or character sketch and a photographic portrait whose edges are blurred.

**Vin blanc/de table/mousseux/rosé/rouge** – wine white, of or for the table (as opposed, one assumes, to wine for cleaning lavatories), 'foaming' (as distinct from *pétillant*, which is lightly sparkling), *rosé* – or pink, through brief contact with the skin of red grapes – and red.

**Vis-à-vis** – literally 'face to face', and thus the name of a carriage in which travellers sat facing one another and also used of a face-to-face meeting, but more generally used as a preposition meaning 'in relation to' or 'with regard to'.

**Vive** – see **Qui vive**. 'Long live …' or 'more power to …', whence we derive such expressions as *vive la bagatelle* ('may frivolity or gibberish thrive') and *vive la différence*, a traditional expression of joy at the differences between the genders.

**Vogue** – fashion, which curiously comes from *voguer*, to row (a boat), so a course or drift.

**Voilà** – literally 'there is …' or 'there are …', but most frequently used in English on its own as an ejaculatory flourish on displaying something or removing it from concealment. It is as though we still felt the need for a good 'Lo!' but cannot bring ourselves to say it, and so have adopted the French form as a substitute. Often rendered, *le voilà!* regardless of the gender of the thing or person displayed.

**Volte face** – a 'U-turn' in policy, strategy or stated opinion. From Latin *volvere* to roll or turn, and *facies*, a face.

**Voyeur** – one who obtains stimulation or gratification by watching others engaged in sexual activities, from *voir*, to see or view.

Needless to say, we are all to a greater or lesser extent *voyeurs*, so the term has meaning only when applied to those for whom this is a fetish, and for whom gratification is unattainable without such stimulus.

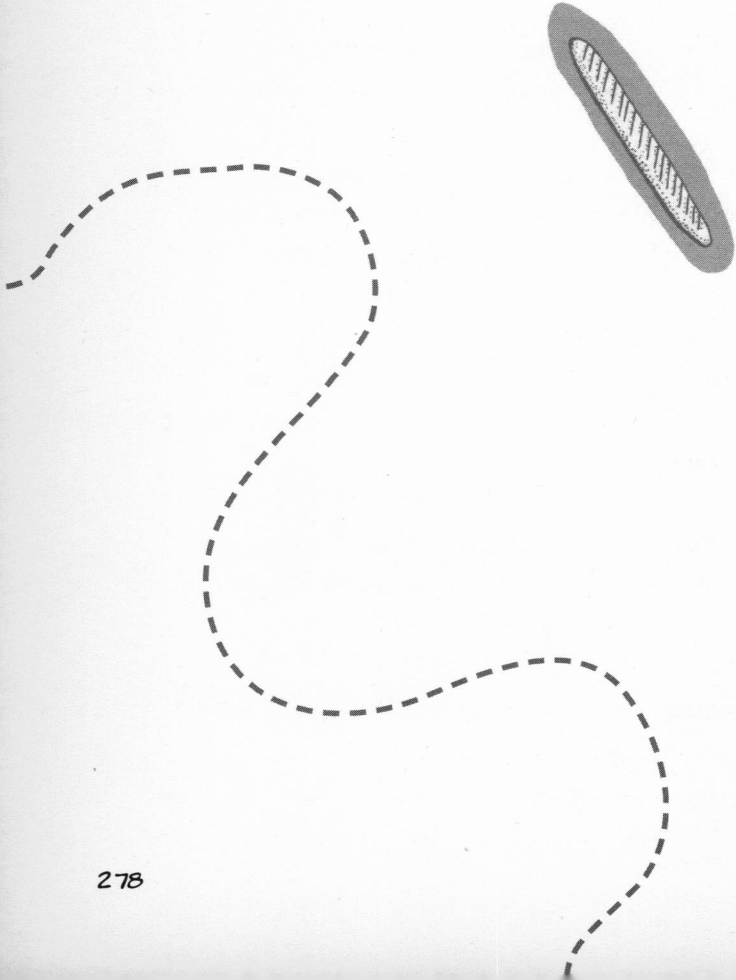